THE RIDGEWAY PATH

Spur Footpath Guides:

- Afoot in Hertfordshire
- Afoot in Surrey
- Walks along Offa's Dyke
- Walks along the Ridgeway
- Walks in Berkshire
- Walks in Buckinghamshire
- Walks in the Cotswolds
- Walks in Devon
- Walks in Hampshire
- Walks in the Lake District
- Walks in Oxfordshire
- Walks in the Surrey Hills
- Walks in Sussex
- Walks in the Yorkshire Dales
- Walks in the Hills of Kent
- Walks in the Peak District
- Afoot in the Yorkshire Dales
- Walks on Exmoor
- Walks in Avon
- Waterside Walks in West London

THE RIDGEWAY PATH

ALAN CHARLES

SPURBOOKS

Published by
SPURBOOKS
(a division of Holmes McDougall Ltd)
Allander House
137-141 Leith Walk
Edinburgh EH6 8NS

Line drawing of the Royal Hotel, Tring Station,
by Richard M. Ridlington, B.A., A.R.I.B.A.
Sketches by Leonard J. Hayes, R.I.B.A.

ISBN 0 7157 2106 2

Royalties from the sale of this book are being donated to TEAR Fund.

CONTENTS

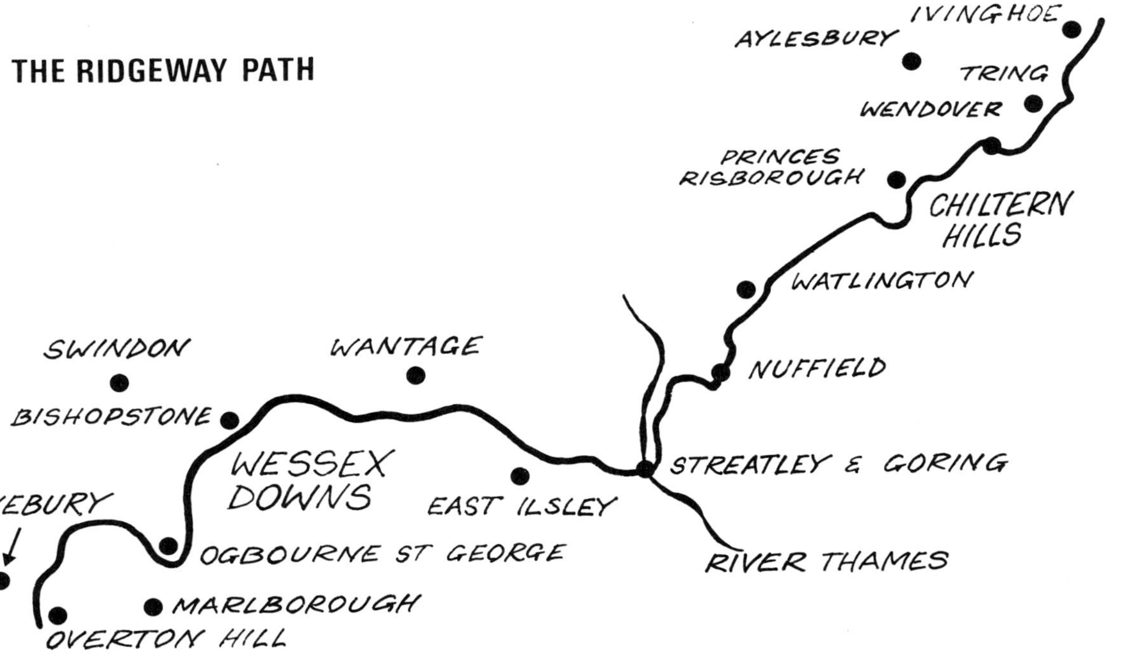
THE RIDGEWAY PATH
IVINGHOE
AYLESBURY
TRING
WENDOVER
PRINCES RISBOROUGH
CHILTERN HILLS
WATLINGTON
NUFFIELD
STREATLEY & GORING
RIVER THAMES
SWINDON
WANTAGE
BISHOPSTONE
WESSEX DOWNS
EAST ILSLEY
AVEBURY
OGBOURNE ST GEORGE
MARLBOROUGH
OVERTON HILL

ACKNOWLEDGEMENTS

I would like to thank my good friends Howard Reeve, Richard Ridlington and Christopher Moss for their help and encouragement, and Mrs Anne Trotman of Chorleywood Field Studies Centre for her advice; also the numerous correspondents who have provided information. My wife, Betty, has helped me enormously – not least in her patient endurance!

I will lift up mine eyes unto the hills from whence
cometh my help.
My help cometh from the Lord, who hath made
heaven and earth.

Psalm 121, verses 1 and 2

Inscription on Baron Wantage's monument on the Ridgeway Path above Wantage.

INTRODUCTION

The Ridgeway – 'greatest, lengthiest and noblest in appearance of all the prehistoric roads' – rides the back of one of the six great ridges that radiate from the central hub of Salisbury Plain. It sails the undulating waves of chalk downland through Wiltshire and Oxfordshire (until recently they were in Berkshire), to the Thames Valley at Goring. This is open, airy country with breathtaking views across the Vale. The way is not wild and barren – as might be supposed from a glance at the map – but punctuated with hedges and small woodlands and homely crops in large fields. Having descended to river level at Goring the ridge reaffirms itself in the north-easterly thrust of the Chiltern escarpment. But the contrast is striking: the escarpment is generously clothed in fine beech woods and indented at near regular intervals with 'gaps' – natural valleys (and one unnatural one, in the case of the M40 motorway through Beacon Hill) carrying important road and rail links. The fields are smaller, the footpaths more numerous, the human population more evident.

Keeping company with the Ridgeway, but at a lower level, is another ancient highway: the Icknield Way. Much of this is a highway in the strictly modern sense, where the interest is not the walking but the delightful villages along the way. From Watlington in Oxfordshire to as far north-east as Ivinghoe in Buckinghamshire it divides into the Upper and Lower Icknield Ways. The Lower Way coincides with the B4009 and other roads over much of its length, while the Upper Way is a trackway running along the foot of the escarpment.

The Ridgeway Path, which runs from Ivinghoe Beacon in Buckinghamshire to Overton Hill in Wiltshire, should not be confused with the 'true' Ridgeway – at least not all of the time. The Path, proposed by the Ramblers Association as long ago as 1942 and brought into being by the Countryside Commission as part of a countrywide network of long-distance routes, follows the Icknield Way for 8 miles (13 km) from Wainhill near Chinnor to a point a mile (1.5 km) north of Swyncombe. Numerous meanderings here and there on well-known and lesser-known paths make up the total Chiltern

ROYAL HOTEL
POSTING HOUSE
RICHARD RIDLINGTON NOV. 1980

contribution to the Ridgeway Path. West of Goring the Path follows the true Ridgeway along much of its length, the main exception being a few miles on low land between Liddington Hill and Barbury Castle in Wiltshire, where the Path instead sweeps south of Ogbourne St George on its way to the Marlborough Downs.

I have divided the guide into eleven 'walks', which in most cases start and finish at towns or villages lying on or close to the Path. In this way the complete Ridgeway Path is covered and you are guided up to and away from it at the beginning and end of each walk. If you add up the distances you will find that you have a total of 95 miles (152 km) to walk whereas the 'official' length of the Path from Ivinghoe Beacon to Overton Hill direct is 85 miles (137 km). The Path throughout its entire length is marked by signposts, concrete plinths and white-painted acorn symbols. Four 1:50,000 series Ordnance Survey maps cover the entire route: these are sheets 165, 173, 174 and 175. If you are fortunate enough to get hold of the earlier one-inch series you will need only three sheets: 157, 158 and 159.

Now for the important matters of transport and accommodation. If you are of the energetic, long-distance, backpacking fraternity you will not be concerned with such matters – except when you need to buy food and when you want to get home at the end of it all. For the rest of us who insist that each day's walking ends pleasantly with good food and a good bed (either at home or away) some careful planning is necessary.

Bus routes are far from ideal and you are well advised to lay your hands on all available timetables (more details in the Appendix and at the end of each chapter); you can then make the most of the very limited services. Given a minimum of one companion and two cars you can, of course, work a simple shuttle system and be entirely independent of public transport.

Depending on your means, accommodation may be less of a problem. There are three well-placed youth hostels: Ivinghoe, Lee Gate (2 miles (3.25 km) south-east of Wendover) and Streatley. Bradenham Hostel, 4½ miles (7.25 km) south of Princes Risborough, is not so well placed but can be reached by bus. A list of accommodation addresses – specially pre-

pared with the Ridgeway Path in mind – may be obtained from the Thames and Chiltern Tourist Board (8 The Market Place, Abingdon, Berkshire). The Ramblers Association *Bed and Breakfast Guide* is an invaluable booklet containing addresses recommended for comfort and good food and is published by the Ramblers Association (1–5 Wandsworth Road, London SW8 2LJ).

Finally, a word for cyclists and riders. The Chiltern section of the Path is generally unsuitable for cycling and riding except along the Icknield Way between Wainhill (above Chinnor) and Swyncombe Downs, 1½ miles (2.5 km) south-east of Watlington. But even the Icknield Way can become a quagmire after heavy rain. The Ridgeway track across the Oxfordshire and Wiltshire Downs is, in the main, ideal for riding; but cycling is another matter: although there are some good stretches, particularly between Streatley and Wantage, the going can be very difficult indeed, with sharp flints and thorns waiting to do their worst. However, a bicycle can be put to good use in alleviating the shortcomings of public transport by giving it a car ride to the point where you intend to finish your day's walking. If it is still there when you arrive you have the straightforward but strenuous task of cycling back by road to your car.

Geology

The Chiltern hills and the downland of Berkshire, Oxfordshire and Wiltshire are vestiges of a landscape of vast domes and ridges formed about 25 million years ago (late in geological time), when lateral forces distorted the earth's crust. The upper strata of these domes and ridges consist of great depths of chalk – many hundreds of feet in places – laid down in the sea 60 million years and more ago.

The precise origin of the chalk is open to debate. Much of it may derive from the breakdown of planktonic algae, although a small part is made up of microscopic fossils. In the lower depths fragments of shells are abundant; in places these constitute the larger part of the bulk. The chalk is classified into Upper, Middle or Lower Chalk, according to depth. The Upper Chalk contains layers of flint. These may have formed in the sea from the solution of siliceous skeletons of fossils or by an inorganic process – that of deposition from sea water. In many places the Upper Chalk is overlaid by what are called 'superficial deposits of clay-with-flints'. The flints were formed within the chalk mass itself but the chalk has since dissolved away through the agency of percolating rainwater, leaving the flints suspended in a less soluble clayey residue.

Prominent features of the Downs, particularly in the region between Marlborough and Avebury in Wiltshire, are the sarsen stones. Otherwise known as bridlestones, Druid stones or greywethers these hard, shapeless stones are scattered over a wide area. They are remnants of a one-time overlying stratum of hard sandstone which has been removed by weathering.

The flints, the sarsens, the chalk: each has played its part in the history of downland man. Flints in the manufacture of primitive weapons and tools, and, over more recent centuries, the construction of buildings and boundary walls; sarsens in the prehistoric stone circles of Avebury and Stonehenge; chalk rock in church and cottage walls.

Wild Flowers

The chalky downland soil supports many flowering plants, some of which – the 'calcicoles' – will grow here (and on limestone soils) but nowhere else. Certain species, though not themselves calcicoles, are well adapted to dry, exposed conditions and are more abundant here than elsewhere. There are many other species that will grow equally well almost anywhere. Only a few of the flowers to be found on chalky soils are mentioned here and my selection is from those most likely to be seen by the casual observer. I find it helpful to divide the chalk habitat into two types: grassland and woodland. 'Grassland' is open, unshaded and in places closely cropped; 'woodland' includes shady places such as field-sides and hedgebanks.

Of the grassland flowers few can rival the beautiful common rockrose: 'clear, cool and yellow on fragile petals'. A flower with a range of colours – pink, white and blue – and in bloom from May until September is the common milkwort. The pea family is well represented: horse-shoe vetch, birdsfoot-trefoil, kidney-vetch, black medick and the restharrow. The horse-shoe vetch is noted for its scent; the restharrow for the way in which it 'arrests' the ploughman's harrow. A serviceable plant is the salad burnet; it was used in such diverse activities as cheese-making and dye manufacture. Then there are the little eyebrights, the most attractive being the common and the large-flowered species. The mouse-ear hawkweed, the field and small scabious and the musk, stemless and carline thistles are members of the daisy family to be found on the Downs. Of the dead-nettle family, self-heal, wild thyme and marjoram are examples. As its name suggests, self-heal was esteemed for its medicinal properties. Wild thyme is well known for the sweetness of its scent. Two orchids to be found in abundance on the grassland are the appropriately named fragrant and pyramidal orchids. Less common is the bee orchid and the autumn lady's tresses.

Included among the earliest woodland flowers are the violets: in particular the wood dog, the hairy and the sweet-scented species. The hairy violet is so named on account of its very hairy leaves; these assist the plant to conserve moisture. The sweet woodruff has been referred to as the 'herb of cordiality' because of its many uses. It was used in wine and to scent linen; and a kind of tea was made from it. Of the more common orchid species to be found in woodland places are the common spotted and butterfly orchids; among others the fly and bird's-nest orchids are less likely to be seen. A common plant with a common name is the wild carrot; in autumn its delicate lacy umbels have the appearance of the birds' nests of the hedgerows.

Birds

As you walk the Ridgeway Path you will see a great variety of bird species: birds of open downland; birds of field, hedgerow and woodland. Since the path is to a great extent a downland route I shall mention here only those species that are characteristic of open, hilly country.

The corn bunting is truly a bird of the wide open spaces. In appearance it is unappealing – a dull streaky brown; its song is often likened to the jangling of a bunch of keys. You should consider yourself fortunate if you see the cirl bunting, for as well as being a shy and secretive bird it is becoming rather scarce. A bird similar in appearance to the cirl bunting is the yellowhammer. It is well known for its song which – given a little imagination – sounds something like 'a little bit of bread and no cheese'.

The wheatear and the whinchat are two delightful summer visitors from the African continent. The wheatear is easily

recognized by its conspicuous white rump. The Victorians gave it special consideration: as a table delicacy. The rare stone-curlew is a bird in a class of its own; it looks much like a wader but is quite at home on heaths and chalk downs. Occasionally included in its courtship display is the amusing habit of thrusting small stones and other objects over its shoulders.

Few are unfamiliar with that delightful aerial songster, the skylark. His sustained musical outpouring is the quintessence of dry hot summer days on cultivated fields and open downs. He is Wordsworth's 'ethereal minstrel' and Shelley's 'blithe spirit'. The meadow pipit is a wide-ranging bird of the open country – of downs, heaths and dunes. You may well stumble upon this bird as you walk the Downs: its nest is built directly on the ground where the eggs run the risk of being trampled underfoot.

You are also likely to see the golden plover during the winter months after it has flown south from its breeding grounds in Scotland. A close relative of the golden plover is the lapwing, popularly known as the peewit on account of its 'song'. He is referred to as the 'farmer's friend' because of his liking for the harmful insects that prey on the farmer's crops.

A game bird you are likely to see is the partridge, particularly where there is good cover in the form of thick grass or bushes. If you flush a partridge from the grass he will despatch himself with a rapid whirring flight. Another game bird that you may be fortunate enough to see is the quail. He is a shy little creature and you are more likely to hear him than see him. Your bird-spotter's book will tell you that the male call is a repeated 'quic . . . quic-ic' (or more imaginatively 'kiss me quick' or 'wet my lips' and the female a repeated 'queep . . . queep'. Both are heard throughout the day and night.

Birds of prey are much less in evidence than in the past and the casual observer may see no more than a kestrel or two on the Downs. There is no novelty in this: the kestrel is Britain's most common day-flying bird of prey. It can be identified by its hovering flight, long tail and pointed wings. A much larger bird of prey, the buzzard, may be seen circling slowly on broad wings high above the Downs. Lying on your back for an hour or so under the warm summer sun is no way to complete the Ridgeway Path but it is a most pleasant and relaxing position from which to observe the buzzard soaring aloft in a blue sky. The rare hobby is also a delight to watch. This 'master of the air' seems (to us at least) to fly for the sheer pleasure of it: gliding, tumbling and looping the loop are part of its breathtaking aerial display.

Roads and Relics

It is thought that the Ridgeway is the oldest existing road in the world. It runs where we would expect the earliest roads to run: along the dry ridge-top where the going was relatively easy, rather than the marshy, densely-wooded vale. The Icknield Way, which came into being later, was clearly a useful compromise between the exposed ridge-top and the marshy vale below: it passes just above the 'spring-line' – that is above the contour where water issues from the foot of the chalk. The Lower Icknield Way between Dunstable and Watlington may have been used more by wheeled traffic as this developed. Throughout historic and prehistoric times the old roads were tramped by all manner of men: cattle drovers, local inhabitants on short journeys between adjacent settlements, long-distance travellers on pilgrimage to the ceremonial centres of Avebury and Stonehenge, and the less desirable marauders and plunderers. With all this activity we are not surprised to see numerous reminders of human occupation along the Ridgeway Path.

Most notable are the Iron Age forts (otherwise known as castles or camps), many of which are situated at strategic points overlooking the vale. Among the best-known forts on or close to the Path are Ivinghoe Beacon, Boddington Hill (overlooking Wendover), Pulpit Hill, Segsbury Down (above Wantage), Whitehorse Hill, Swinley Down (Alfred's Castle), Liddington Hill, Marlborough Downs (Barbury Castle). In general all you will see at these sites is a single rampart and ditch enclosing a large area of land.

Five hill figures accompany the route of the Ridgeway Path. They are cut into the thin turf – exposing the chalk – and are seen from considerable distances. Along the Chiltern section there is Whiteleaf Cross above Princes Risborough, Bledlow Cross above Chinnor and the White Mark above Watlington. In Berkshire the magnificent White Horse of Uffington overlooks the Vale of the White Horse; in Wiltshire the Hackpen Horse lies along the west-facing slope of the Marlborough Downs. At many places along the Path you will see sections of the extensive bank and ditch known as Grim's Ditch or Dyke – sweeping 'like a green bridge' across country. Opinions differ about the age and purpose of the dyke: Iron Age, Roman, Saxon; civil boundary or defensive rampart.

There seem to be more reminders of the death of prehistoric man than the activities of his life. His burial mounds or barrows (marked as 'tumuli' on the Ordnance Survey map) are scattered over a wide area. Long barrows belong to the Neolithic period (New Stone Age) while round barrows are usually of the Bronze Age. The round barrow is classified as either bowl, bell, disc, pond or saucer depending on its shape. The last few miles of the Path pass through an area of particular archaeological interest; an area that was a centre of intensive human occupation during Neolithic times. Here is the stone circle of Avebury, the massive mound of Silbury Hill and the West Kennett long barrow – all within walking distance of the 'end' of the Ridgeway Path.

A Note for Energetic Walkers

Points of departure from the route of the Ridgeway Path are marked in numerical sequence in the text. This is for the convenience of those who are walking two (or more) sections in one go. For example, when walking all the way from Ivinghoe to Wendover in one day you should ignore the text between **(1)** in the first walk to **(2)** in the second. Where the end of one walk and the start of the next coincide exactly with the Ridgeway Path *no* numbers are given.

Extra care is needed when approaching the end of the East Ilsley–Wantage section, where things get rather complicated. The numbering appears to go completely crazy (for example **(10)** appears at the end of the next section instead of the beginning) but if you keep strictly to numerical sequence by jumping from **(9)** to **(10)** all will be well.

Chapter 1

IVINGHOE BEACON TO TRING

6 miles (9.5 km)

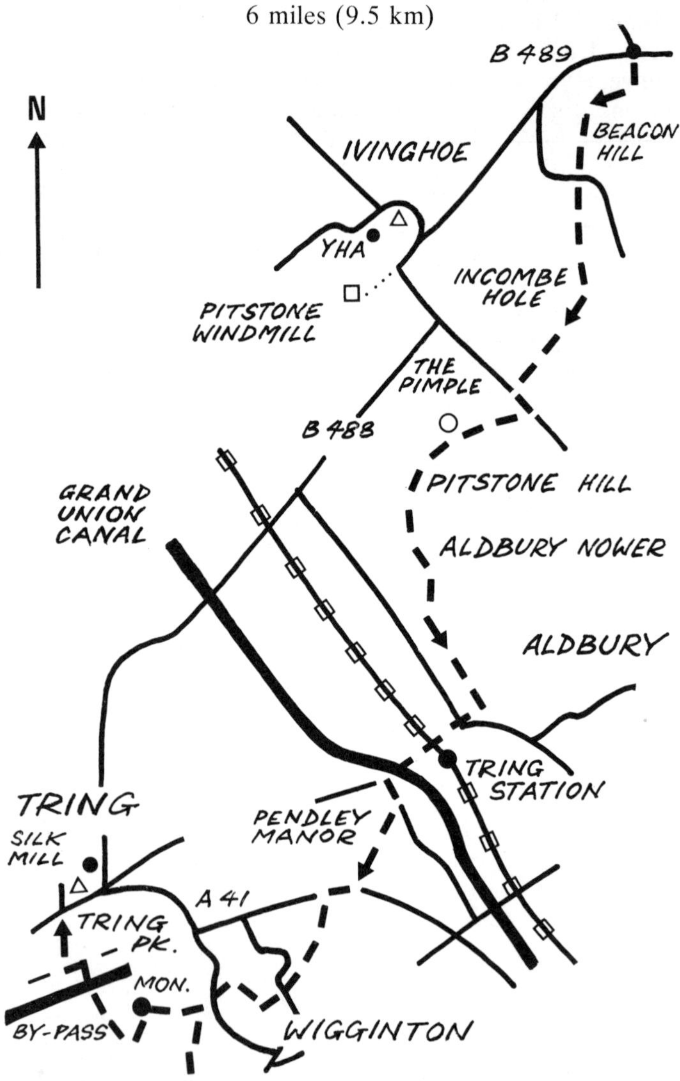

The Ridgeway Path starts at the summit of Ivinghoe Beacon (Beacon Hill) and follows the open downland as far as Pitstone Hill. After passing through Aldbury Nower Wood it descends to Tring Station and the Grand Union Canal in the Bulbourne Valley. It then rises to Wigginton and Tring Park, where we leave the official route and go down through the lovely wooded park to Tring itself.

Since you may have the good sense to stop at Ivinghoe before starting the walk a few words about this pleasant little village may be of interest. In the village centre the imposing eighteenth-century Old Brewery House serves as the youth hostel. Next door is the Old Town Hall, now the public library and looking a little neglected. Cathedral-like St Mary's Church stands close by. Although it 'suffered some outrage' in 1871 in the name of 'restoration', there remains much to delight the eye – in particular the fine fifteenth-century roof. An enormous thatch-hook is attached to the churchyard wall; this was used to drag thatch from cottage roofs to prevent the spread of fire. Opposite the church is the seventeenth-century King's Head Hotel with a very cosy-looking restaurant. Nearby Vicarage Lane has some charming old cottages – and the Rose and Crown pub.

Pitstone Windmill is well worth a visit. It stands in a field ¼ mile (0.5 km) south of Ivinghoe just off the B488 road. Built in 1627 (or so an inscription seems to indicate) it is probably the oldest remaining windmill in England. In 1902, only seven years after extensive repairs were carried out, a freak storm badly damaged the mill. It was not worked again commercially and remained derelict until 1937 when it was offered to the National Trust by Leonard Hawkins of nearby Pitstone Green Farm. Some repairs were put in hand at that time but complete restoration was not started until 1963.

The best point from which to ascend Beacon Hill is at the junction of the B489 with the Ivinghoe–Aston road, 1¼ miles (2 km) north-east of Ivinghoe village (grid reference 963172). There is a lay-by here and a wide verge where cars can be parked; also a bus stop for the number 61 route. Before you start walking, a word or two about Beacon Hill: the turf on the hill is stamped out by innumerable feet every sunny weekend and the paths have become badly eroded. Although my directions will take you along the main path over the hill a liberal interpretation would help to conserve the thin soil.

A few steps from the lay-by, in the direction of Ivinghoe, a footpath sign directs you uphill through thorn bushes towards Beacon Hill. The path soon runs up alongside a wire fence bordering a field on the left. At the top of the path (there is a rail in the wire fence on the left) turn right and go ahead to the summit of Beacon Hill. An Ordnance Survey plinth and a vandalized direction indicator stand at the top; there is also the mound of a bowl barrow. Now, having taken your fill of the view, which includes Whipsnade Zoo with its white lion cut into the hillside, you should turn left through the middle of the barrow (or better still, *around* it) and descend the spur of the hill on what soon becomes a chalky path all the way down to a road. On the way down you will have crossed the faintly visible rampart of an Iron Age fort that surrounded the hill; you will see this clearly later on as a notch in the hillside. The second hillock on the right, the shoulder of which interrupts the steady drop of the path, is capped by a bowl barrow.

Cross the road to the widest of the paths opposite. Follow this path to its summit on Steps Hill and then downhill to a stile and gate. Here the path skirts the left-hand rim of a deep coombe called Incombe Hole. Some 474 acres of land hereabouts is classified as a Site of Special Scientific Interest – partly on account of the chalk grassland. Stay on this path as it curves right and slopes downhill to a stile leading into a field beyond the coombe. Follow the path across the field, with a wire fence left, for ⅓ mile (0.5 km) to the Aldbury–Ivinghoe road. Turn left on to this and, after 100 yards (90 m), go through a gate leading into a small car park on the right-hand side of the road. Go straight ahead over a stile and along a path with a wire fence and field immediately to your left. Keep near to the fence all the way up the broad slope of the hill (Pitstone Hill).

The hillock that you will pass to your right is appropriately named 'the Pimple' and should not be confused with Pitstone Hill. However, it does make an interesting diversion – especially for the children. The view from the Pimple takes in the cement works and chalk-pits, Ivinghoe village, Pitstone Windmill, and the distant waters of Tring reservoirs. The reservoirs, in addition to feeding the summit of the Grand Union Canal, are well known for their bird life; the banks and surrounding woodlands constitute a National Nature Reserve.

There is much of archaeological interest here on Pitstone Hill. Lower down the hill, in the general direction of the cement works, are the pits of old – probably Neolithic – flint workings. It is well worth making a diversion here for the wild flowers; they seem to enjoy this miniature landscape of undulating 'hills'. There is also evidence of an Iron Age settlement and field system, a Roman well, a pagan Saxon burial site, a medieval house, and a section of Grim's Dyke. So it is not surprising that the hill has been designated a Site of Special Scientific Interest.

Continue following the fence as it curves left over the hill, and, when you are within 100 yards (90 m) of a wood ahead, bear right – downhill – to a stile leading into a wood (Aldbury Nowers). The path now follows the line of Grim's Dyke, firstly under a stand of beech trees and then deeper into the wood ahead. After a short walk (about ¼ mile (0.5 km)) the level woodland path arrives at a clearing. *Now be careful:* follow the level path *across* the clearing – *not* the half-left uphill path. The path meets Grim's Dyke again and re-enters the wood. A crossing track is soon reached; turn right here and follow the track as it curves left and downhill. At the point where the track bears right and continues downhill under some chestnut trees (to a road) you must turn left along a path that follows the top left-hand border of a field (with small trees and scrub on your left). Continue along this path until you pass a new building (Westland Farm) on your right. There are some large beech trees lining the path at this point. Immediately after passing the farm you should turn right and go down the farm drive to the road.

You should normally turn right on to the road but, if you have time to spare, I recommend that you turn left and walk the mile (1.5 km) to the village of Aldbury. The village, with its delightful sixteenth- and seventeenth-century cottages, ancient stocks and village pond, lies at the foot of the wooded slopes of Aldbury Common. Good tea can be had at one of the old cottages, so it is worth going that extra mile!

Now back to Westland Farm: on leaving the drive you will need to go down the road to Tring Station and the Grand Union Canal. The station itself is at the southern end of the famous Tring cutting. Built between 1834 and 1838 to carry the London–Birmingham line through the Chilterns, the cutting is 2½ miles (4 km) long and 57 feet (17 m) deep for a ¼ mile (0.4 km). The station itself was regarded as first class' and boasted 'one inspector, three policemen, four porters, and one stationary-engine man'.

When you cross the canal you will see that it too has a deep cutting to take it through the Chiltern escarpment. This is 1½ miles (2 km) long and 30 feet (9 m) deep at one point, and was completed in 1797 as part of what was then known as the Grand Junction Canal. The 3-mile (4.8-km) summit level of the canal extends in both directions from this crossing; it is fed with water from reservoirs situated 2 miles (3 km) or so to the north-west, near Marsworth. Many improvements have been made over the years in an effort to increase the amount of available water, but this has resulted in a very complex system. Now the British Waterways Board have repaired and renovated this stretch of the canal – from Northchurch to Marsworth – with the object of promoting public and government interest in the national canal network.

After crossing the canal, turn left immediately and follow the road for 200 yards (180 m) to an iron gate on the right-hand side. Strike across the field (between fences) to the near left-hand corner of a wood and follow the right-hand edge of a field with the wood immediately to your right. The wood borders Pendley Manor, which is used as a College of Adult Education. An old record states that Pendley was 'a great town' in the fifteenth century and that there were in the town '13 plows besides divers handicraft men'. In 1448 Sir Robert Whittingham of Pendley Manor razed the town, ploughed up the land and laid it down to pasture.

In ⅓ mile (0.5 km) you will reach the A41 road; turn right on to this and go along it for about 100 yards (90 m). Cross the A41 and head for the stile opposite, signposted 'The Twist'. Follow the iron fence uphill – crossing two stiles at the unfinished end of a motorway – until you approach some beech trees near the top. A stile in the iron fence on your left leads you into the bottom right-hand corner of a large field. Follow the field's right-hand edge to a stile in its far right-hand corner. The stile connects you to a lane. Turn right for 20 yards (18 m) to a stile on the left-hand side. Go over this and then along a narrow path between parallel wire fences. After two stiles the path soon turns right, leading you into a field. Follow the right-hand edge of the field to a stile in its far right-hand corner. Then forward between parallel wire fences; these lead you past an Ordnance Survey plinth along the upper edge of a field to join a road at the field's far left-hand corner – adjacent to a house with 'Tudor' chimneys. Here is the village of Wigginton. Cross the road to a short drive opposite. The drive serves some houses on the left-hand side and ends at the entrance to Tring Park (**1**). Now we leave the Ridgeway Path and go down through lovely Tring Park to Tring itself. To continue on the Path, turn now to (**2**) on page 28.

Henry Guy enclosed the park after Tring Manor was granted to him by Charles II. The enclosure met with much opposition from the 'poor of the parish' who lost part of Wigginton Common in the process. The park was extended in the eighteenth century by Sir William Gore. In 1950 Alison Uttley wrote: 'Will Tring keep its supreme beauty, which is the Park? . . . no park that ever I saw excels it.' The busy Tring bypass now thrusts its rude course through this fine place. Go through the gate into the wood. At the first crossing path go slightly right and downhill to a junction of paths at an obelisk. This was erected in memory of Charles II's mistress Nell Gwynne (or her dog). Tradition has it that 'pretty, witty Nell' had a house here in the park, and if you will send your children hopping backwards around the obelisk she will give them each an orange!

Turn left at the obelisk into the downhill path (not the level one) leading to an iron gate and stile where the wood begins to clear. Turn right here and go downhill between wire fences into a shallow valley and straight on to cross the motorway by a footbridge. The impressive mansion ahead of you retains little of the house designed by Sir Christopher Wren for Henry Guy. This was enclosed within a much larger building following the purchase of the Manor by Baron Lionel Rothschild in 1872. Today the house is in the good hands of the Arts Educational School.

Having crossed the bypass go along a narrow path to Park Street. Turn left for Tring Zoological Museum. This houses an outstanding collection of specimens including mammals, birds, reptiles and fishes. It is now just a short walk along Akeman Street to the town centre. The town was once an important centre for lace and straw plait making, cottage industries which are now largely extinct. It also boasted a silk mill with the largest water wheel in Hertfordshire – 22 feet (6.7 m) in diameter. The mill buildings can be seen from Brook Street.

Returning to Ivinghoe and Beacon Hill

Bus 61: an hourly service; two-hourly on Sunday.
Taxis: 5878 Private Hire Co., telephone: Tring 5878; D. L. Gilson, telephone: Tring 2705.

Staying in Ivinghoe and Tring

Ivinghoe Youth Hostel (closed most Mondays), telephone: Cheddington 668251.
Accommodation and camp-site at Silver Birch Café, Pitstone, telephone: Cheddington 668348.
Henekeys (ex Rose and Crown), Tring, telephone: Tring 4071.
Royal Hotel, Tring Station, telephone: Tring 2169, (on the Ridgeway Path 1½ miles (2.4 km) from Tring).

Eating in Ivinghoe and Tring

Ivinghoe: The Kings Head Restaurant; Silver Birch Café, Pitstone (¾ mile (1.2 km) from Ivinghoe); The Bell.
Tring: The Bell, High Street; Foxy's Corner House, Frogmore Street; Trattoria Pinocchio, High Street.

Chapter 2

TRING TO WENDOVER

7 miles (11.25 km)

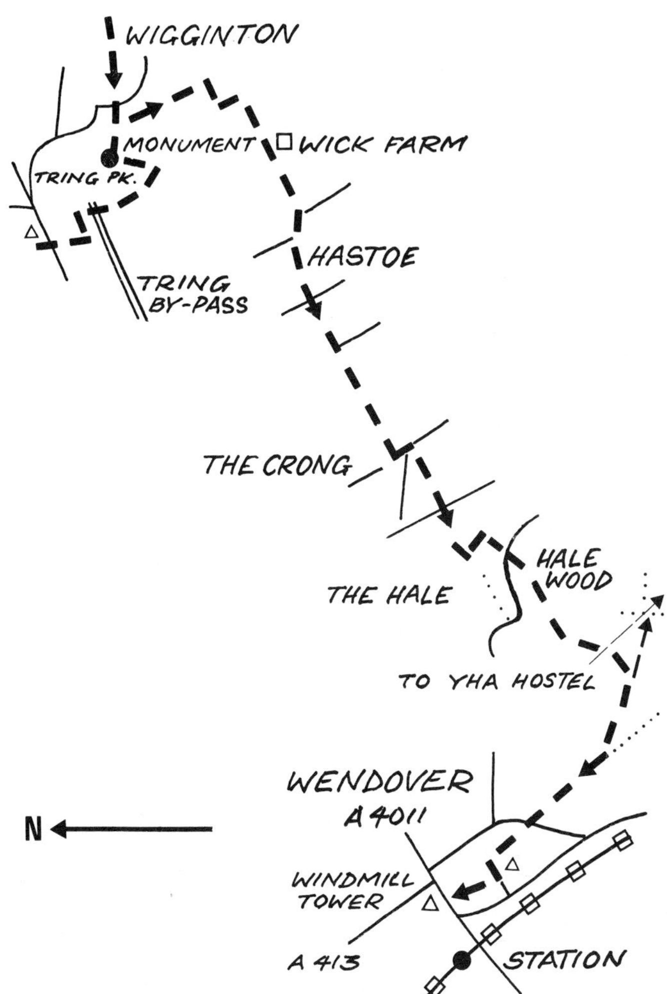

Before meeting the Ridgeway Path at Wigginton today's route crosses the Tring bypass and ascends the wooded slope of Tring Park. The Path then runs along the border between Tring Park and Wigginton's back gardens. Beyond Wigginton lie Hastoe, Wendover Forest and beautiful Hale Woods, with fine views across Wendover Gap and the Vale of Aylesbury.

The A41 road through the centre of Tring is met by Akeman Street 200 yards (180 m) west of the church. Go along Akeman Street and turn left into Park Street alongside the Zoological Museum. At a tile-hung house 200 yards (180 m) along Park Street turn right into a path signposted 'Tring Park and Wigginton'. This takes you between wire fences to the footbridge crossing the Tring bypass. Having crossed the bypass follow the left-hand edge of the field for a few yards – with the bypass on your left – and then bear half-right across the park towards the distant wooded slope. You will go down into a shallow valley and up between parallel wire fences to meet the wood. The Mansion House is in view behind you (see page 26). Immediately you enter the wood turn left at a gate and stile and go uphill along a woodland drive to meet a junction of ways at Nell Gwynne's obelisk (see page 25). Here you must make a 90 degrees right turn (*not* acutely right) into a narrow uphill path. At the next crossing drive keep straight on along the level path which soon leads you to a gate and out into the open. Turn right immediately along a narrow path running between a house and the wood (**2**).

You are now on the Ridgeway Path and at the start of a long stretch that follows Wigginton's back gardens. There is an iron gate after a few yards and the path widens. A drive is crossed and the path continues to follow the back gardens. The path turns sharp right near cedar trees and soon opens out into a field at a stile. Turn left and follow the field's left-hand border until you reach a flinty track. Turn right in the track and follow it for ¾ mile (1.2 km) – passing Wick Farm en route – to a road. Go forward to a T-junction and follow the road signposted to Hastoe. You will pass Hastoe Cross Cottage on your right almost immediately. Keep straight on through Hastoe (which consists of little more than a few farm buildings) and, where the road turns sharp left ¼ mile (0.4 km) further, go off half-right into Pavis Wood and continue in the same direction as before. This woodland path is about ¾ mile (1.2 km) long and for most of its length is not more than a few yards from the left-hand extremity of the wood.

The path leaves the wood at its far left-hand corner at the summit of a steep narrow road. Turn left on to this and walk ahead for a few yards. Immediately after passing an aerial mast on your left, go half-right over a stile in the corner of a field. (The field is bounded along its right-hand edge by a gravel track serving a few bungalows; to the left of the stile there are some low farm buildings.) Cross the field diagonally to a stile at the near right-hand corner of a small rectangular conifer plantation. Go over this and follow the right-hand edge of the plantation, which soon merges into a hedge. Where the hedge turns left bear slightly left across the field to a stile at a road.

Cross the road to a lane opposite and follow this into Wendover Woods. The wood is one of the Forestry Commission's many forest parks with routes laid out for horse-riders and walkers, car parks, picnic areas and 'viewpoints'. The highest point of the Chilterns is in this wood. The O.S. map shows a spot-height of 857 feet (261 m) on the road just crossed. The path ahead leads you alongside beech trees; as it descends the hill and sinks between high banks, it is accompanied by woodland on each side. *Do not go* blindly on all the way downhill (it is tempting – I know); when a clearing appears on your left-hand side you should turn left, scramble out of the sunken path, and go uphill to meet a wire fence at the upper extremity of a large field. Your view down-field includes a huddle of cottages and farm buildings at The Hale, set against the backcloth of the Wendover Gap. After following the curve of the wire fence for about 100 yards (90 m) continue uphill and go right with the path at the top edge of the wood. After about ¼ mile (0.4 km) the path ends at a narrow road. Go just a few steps downhill and join a track on the left which runs through Hale Wood.

After you have walked a short distance from the road you will see a narrow path going downhill through the undergrowth. If you descend this path for just a few yards you will be rewarded with a view of The Hale beautifully laid out at the foot of Wendover Woods. But do not get carried away: that was just a diversion. Back on the track, which dips and curves here and there, you will eventually come out above an area of younger trees. The distant break in the Chiltern escarpment is the Wendover Gap, opening out to the Vale of Aylesbury. Immediately after a stile and gate ahead turn left and follow the path along the edge of the wooded coombe to a T-junction. Turn right here and follow the path downhill. Ignore the track going off half-left after 200 yards (180 m) and turn right at a T-junction after a further 100 yards (90 m). (The narrow waymarked path on the left soon after this T-junction is for those who are bound for the youth hostel; further details at the end of the chapter.)

Continue all the way downhill to meet a track at the bottom. Go ahead along this and turn right just beyond an old orchard. You will soon pass Boswells Farm opposite a fine avenue of beech trees. *Do not go* down there but *continue* along the track, which evolves into a made-up lane, for ½ mile (0.8 km) until you come to a crossroads, passing a farm on the left. Boddington Hill is over to your right. Hidden among trees on this spur of Wendover Woods is the site of an Iron Age fort.

At the crossroads go over to Church Lane opposite and follow this to St Mary's Church. If you choose to nip down the drive just before the church your reward will be a fine view of the Manor House, now part of a school. St Mary's Church is ½ mile (0.8 km) from the centre of Wendover. The story goes that witches or fairies carried away the building materials from what would have been a site closer to Wendover. Inside there is a plaque commemorating one William Bradshawe, his wife, nine children and 23 grandchildren – but you will have to take my word for it because the church, having suffered vandalism, is now open only during services.

Turn right into Heron Path, opposite the lych-gate of the church, and follow it past a large pond and a playground on the left. The path passes Sluice Cottage and runs alongside a stream to meet a lane. Cross the lane to the path opposite and, passing the garden of a large house on the right, go ahead to Wendover High Street. Robert Louis Stevenson's oft-quoted phrase 'a straggling, purposeless sort of place' is unlikely to gain a sympathetic hearing today. A busy place certainly – the Icknield Way passes through the centre and carries heavy

traffic – but straggling and purposeless – no! Those who find pleasure in old buildings will be delighted with it. In the High Street there is the Two Brewers, some two hundred years old, the Red Lion (where it is thought Cromwell and Stevenson stayed), sixteenth-century Bosworth House (now the Post Office) and, at the lower end of the High Street, the clock tower (1842). Then there is eighteenth-century Vine Tree House in Back Street and Lime Tree House in Pound Street, and just around the corner in Aylesbury Road an attractive terrace of old houses. A sail-less windmill tower stands just off Aylesbury Road. The mill was first put into operation in 1804. The cap is said to be the largest in England and the tower one of the tallest. Its walls are three feet thick at the base. The sails were taken down in 1904 after being damaged in a storm, and the mill driven by steam until 1926. The tower is now a private house.

Diversion from Hale Wood to Lee Gate Youth Hostel

Leave the Ridgeway Path along a narrow waymarked path going off to the left just after the second T-junction. Follow this up for a few yards to a track. Turn left along this and go straight ahead, ignoring a left-hand branch and then a right-hand branch. When the path becomes indistinct keep more or less straight ahead. Turn right when you meet a crossing track. This leads to a stile and out into a large field. Follow the left-hand edge of the field to another stile in its far left-hand corner. Turn right in the track and proceed to a road. Turn left along the road for the youth hostel.

Returning to Tring

Bus 366 to Halton Camp (every 20 minutes Monday–Saturday, two-hourly Sunday), then Bus 72 to Tring (Monday–Friday only, 16.47 only) or walk the tow-path of the Grand Union Canal, Wendover branch.

Taxis: Philbys, telephone: Wendover 622195; Wendover Car Hire, telephone: Wendover 624094.

Staying in Wendover

Red Lion Hotel, High Street, telephone: Wendover 622266.

Mrs Fitzgerald, 91 Aylesbury Road, telephone: Wendover 623588.

Mrs Y. MacDonald, 46 Lionel Avenue, telephone: Wendover 623426.

Youth Hostel at Lee Gate (½ mile (0.8 km) from the Ridgeway Path; 2 miles (3.2 km) from Wendover) (closed Tuesdays), telephone: The Lee 395.

Eating in Wendover

The Landon, South Street; Anne Boleyn, Pound Street; Spinning Wheel Restaurant, Aylesbury Road.

Chapter 3

WENDOVER TO PRINCES RISBOROUGH

6 miles (9.5 km)

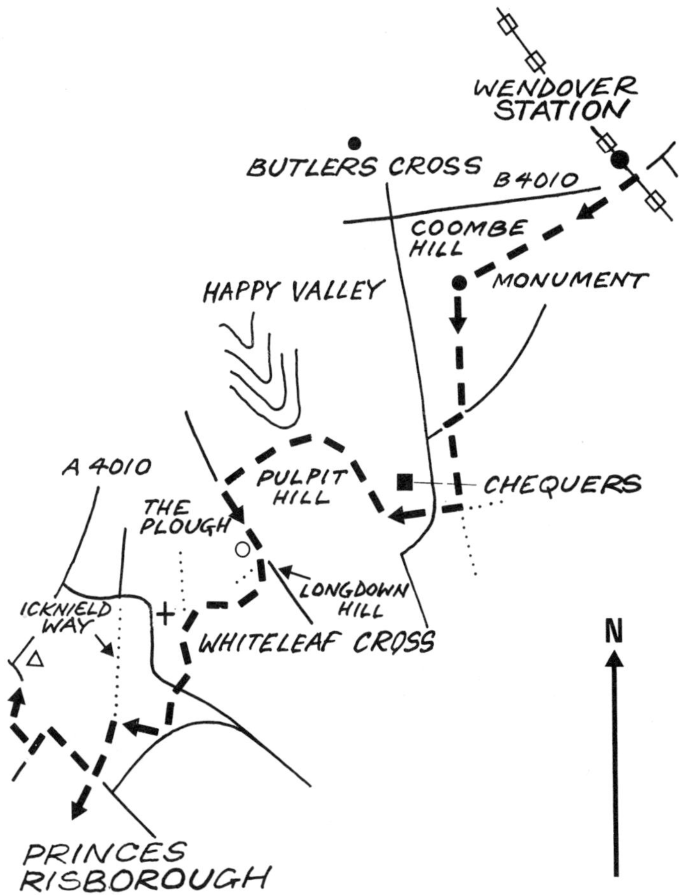

These few miles are amongst the most beautiful along the Ridgeway Path. First we ascend the 842-ft (257-m) Coombe Hill, beloved of walkers and picnickers; then through fine beech woods to the Chequers estate and on to the popular region of scrub and grassland below Pulpit Hill. After climbing the steep wooded slope of Whiteleaf Hill to Whiteleaf Cross we descend to Princes Risborough. For a complete round trip in one day you could, after arrival at Princes Risborough, take bus 323/324 to Kimble or Butler's Cross and walk to Wendover along the path running almost parallel to the B4010 Upper Icknield Way. You should not omit a visit to Little Kimble Church, for here you will see some remarkable fourteenth-century wall paintings.

From Wendover's Pound Street, which is the continuation of High Street, go over the railway bridge into Ellesborough Road. Then, passing some cottages on the right, go up to the sharp bend in the road; leave the road here and join a path starting from the left-hand side. The path divides into two ways almost immediately; take the right-hand path – the one with the stile – uphill through the trees, ignoring left- and right-hand branches. The trees soon recede and you are out on to undulating sward accompanied for some distance by a grassy ditch; there is a flight of steps to help you on your way. This is good country for birds, wild flowers, blackberries and picnics! The view across the Aylesbury Plain soon opens up: a notable landmark is Weston Turville reservoir beyond the northern extremity of Wendover. It was built to supply water to the mills at Aylesbury but later used to feed the Tring–Wendover canal. It now functions as an important bird habitat and is a Nature Reserve of the Berkshire, Buckinghamshire and Oxfordshire Naturalists' Trust (BBONT).

Advancing uphill you cross three fences before reaching the 842-ft (257-m) summit of Coombe Hill, the highest viewpoint in the Chilterns (which should not be confused with the highest point, which is 3 miles (4.8 km) away in Wendover Woods). Here the chalk grassland, heath and woodland are included in a Site of Special Scientific Interest. The hill was given to the National Trust in 1918 by Lord and Lady Lee of Fareham. The monument commemorates the Boer War. In 1938 it was almost completely destroyed by lightning; the

granite blocks were flung nearly as far as the golf course below. A similar but less dramatic incident occurred recently. It goes without saying that there is much to see from this elevated position. I am told that St Paul's Cathedral is numbered on the list, but I have my doubts. Ellesborough Church stands ½ mile (0.8 km) westward overlooked by the promontory of Beacon Hill. Massingham's opinion was that the church has been 'wickedly vulgarized inside'; it might be worth visiting on that account alone. The church does, however, have the distinction of having been attended at its services by certain national leaders during their brief visits to nearby Chequers, the prime minister's country home. Chequers is in view some ¾ mile (1.2 km) to the south-west; but more of that later.

Turn left at the monument and pass to the right of a line of gorse and thorn, with the golf course down below on your right. Stay more or less at this level until you approach a wire fence running downhill. Now *do not* go over the stile directly ahead, but *bear left* to a stile under trees higher up in the fence. Cross the stile into a beech wood and go straight ahead with a field just to your left. After about ¼ mile (0.4 km) you will arrive at a road with a flint cottage opposite. Turn right in the road and go down for 200 yards (180 m) to a track on the left. Take the right-hand branch of this track almost immediately and follow this into the wood. Branch right again after a few hundred yards and follow the waymarked trees. A field comes into view on the right and the level route bears right before meeting a junction of sunken ways. Keep straight on and then turn right at a crossing track ahead. Go downhill over a wide crossing track and then go straight on – with fields right and left – to the road at Buckmoorend, which you will find overlooks the Chequers estate.

Chequers has been much altered and enlarged since its original construction, which was probably in the 1560s. It was given to the nation by Lord Lee of Fareham in 1917 to be used as a retreat for the prime minister. David Lloyd George was the first to take up residence, but he – like his successor Bonar Law – did not altogether welcome the opportunity. Later prime ministers have shown more appreciation. Winston Churchill made good use of Chequers during his term of office in the Second World War; it was his 'power house of strategy'.

You should cross the road at Buckmoorend to the stepped stile opposite and follow the clearly marked path across the park. This replaces an earlier, most direct, route which was closed in the interests of security. You will cross the main drive about 100 yards (90 m) from the lodge gates. This is known as Victory Drive and was planted with beech trees by Sir Winston Churchill. The path then crosses a field and heads uphill to a stile at the left-hand corner of a wood (Mable Wood). It turns right here and follows the edge of the wood for about ⅓ mile (0.5 km) to a stile on the left.

Now you must be careful: cross the stile and strike across the *centre* of the next field keeping the woods on your left- and right-hand at equal distances – for the first few yards at least. After passing the right-hand side of a few isolated trees, go forward along the rising path to a stile adjacent to an iron gate and straight on to the head of a deep coombe. The coombe has the delightful name Happy Valley and is part of a BBONT nature reserve and a Site of Special Scientific Interest. While it is a haven for an interesting collection of plants and animals its primary distinction is that it is thought to be one of only three natural boxwoods in England. After passing the coombe the path divides into two ways; take the uppermost branch, which, after a few yards, cuts across a ditch. There are a number of these 'linear ditches' hereabouts; their origins are uncertain, but it is likely they are associated with the Iron Age fort on Pulpit Hill.

A small rounded hill called Chequers Knap lies ahead of you; go past the left-hand side of this to a stile under trees. Then go downhill along a sunken path for a few yards and turn half-left into a short, narrow path through bushes to a stile. Now go straight ahead along a chalky path (the butts of an old firing range are in the distance on your left), which soon runs beside a wire fence below a beech wood. The wood reaches up and over Pulpit Hill on which is the Iron Age fort mentioned above. Ignore the first stile in the fence and continue ahead to a second stile at the point where the wire fence turns sharply right. Go over the stile and continue walking in the same direction as previously. Now *take care: turn right* at the next crossing path – beside a Nature Reserve sign board – and left after 20 yards (18 m) through a gap in the hedge. You will soon join a path coming in from the left. Go right with this and then bear left into a field.

The area of scrub and grassland well over to your left is known as Grange Lands and is another Nature Reserve managed by BBONT. Grange Lands is freely open to the public and is noted for its rich variety of wild flowers, butterflies and birds. Cross the field diagonally to a coniferous wood at the far end. The path enters the wood about 100 yards (90 m) from the field's far right-hand corner and plunges steeply down between wire fences to a road. Turn left in the road (this is the lower part of Longdown Hill) and follow this up to a side road (Cadsdean Road) in which stands The Plough. Stop here for a ploughman's lunch and choose from no less than twelve varieties of cheese!

Turn right into a bridleway immediately beyond The Plough; after a few yards you must leave the bridleway by turning half-left into a beech wood. The woodland path soon divides two ways; take the right-hand branch (the steepest) and go uphill along what becomes – near the summit – a very steep climb. This is Whiteleaf Hill.

At the summit the trees open out and you can look down on Princes Risborough. The green heights of Wainhill occupy the middle distance while the thin hazy line of the 'Berkshire'

Downs projects along the horizon. Directly in front of you, almost hidden from view on the steep downward slope, is Whiteleaf Cross carved out of the chalk. As with many other hill figures, the Cross is steeped in mystery and controversy. Of the many theories propounded, the one I prefer (illogically, perhaps) states that the pyramid base was cut by prehistoric man as a landmark for the traveller and the Cross added as a devotional symbol in Christian times. At the top of the hill, just above the Cross and to one side, a small group of ash trees marks the site of a Neolithic barrow. This was excavated in the 1930s by Sir Lindsay Scott. A timber burial chamber and the scattered remains of a middle-aged man were found here; also numerous flint implements and fragments of pottery, on which impressions of cultivated cereal grains were found. Another, smaller, mound can be seen a few steps northwards beside a grassy path. This one has a cross impressed upon it and may be the site of a former windmill (a refreshing change from burial mounds!).

Standing with the Cross ahead and below you, you should turn left and go along the level path through the woods (ignoring two right-hand branches) all the way to a car park and picnic area. Drop down to the road here, turn right and go along the road for a few yards to a concrete drive going tangentially off to the left and uphill. After passing through a gate at the top of the slope follow the drive round to the left until it comes to an abrupt end. Keeping the woods to your left go ahead, across a stile and on between the woods and a single line of trees. Then bear right to a stile at a road.

Now *do not* go into the road but make a 90 degrees right-hand turn to cross the open hillside in the general direction of Princes Risborough. If you have judged that 90 degrees turn correctly and have not followed the downward road too closely, you will meet a stile lower down on the slope of the hill. On the other side of the stile is a path which drops downhill amongst thorn scrub, goes over a crossing path and meets, at a stile, the top left-hand corner of a sloping field.

The steeple of Princes Risborough Church should now be directly ahead of you. Follow the wire fence down to a stile; this leads you into another field and down on to a track – the Upper Icknield Way itself. Turn left in this and go with it until it meets a road. Turn right at the road and you will soon be in Princes Risborough (**3**). To continue on the Path turn to (**4**) on page 41.

'Untidy Metroland below the Chilterns' is how John Betjeman saw Princes Risborough. This may be true of the town as a whole but not – to my mind – of the confines of Church Street and High Street. The lovely old Market House stands at the focal point of these two streets and is still used by stallholders on market days. Seventeenth-century Cromwell House in Church Street has been rescued from a state of dilapidation and thoroughly restored by Buckinghamshire County Council. This has earned it a Scheme of Merit placing in the European Architectural Heritage Year awards. The red-brick Mansion House opposite the church is in the care of the National Trust and is open to the public.

Returning to Wendover

Bus 323/324 to Kimble or Butler's Cross (half-hourly on weekdays, two-hourly Sunday) then walk 3 miles (4.8 km) to Wendover (2 miles (3.2 km) from Butler's Cross) via Wellwick Farm.

Taxis: Venture Cars, telephone: Princes Risborough 6559; Witcher Bros, telephone: Princes Risborough 4239.

Staying in Princes Risborough

George and Dragon Hotel, High Street, telephone: Princes Risborough 3087.

Black Prince Hotel, Wycombe Road, telephone: Princes Risborough 5569.

Youth Hostel at Bradenham (4½ miles (7.2 km)), telephone: Naphill 2929 (bus 321 from Princes Risborough; three-hourly Monday–Friday). Limited opening (see YHA Handbook).

Eating in Princes Risborough

Indian Restaurant, High Street; The Pepper Pot, Duke Street; Fish Restaurant, Market Square.

Chapter 4

PRINCES RISBOROUGH TO WATLINGTON

11½ miles (18.5 km)

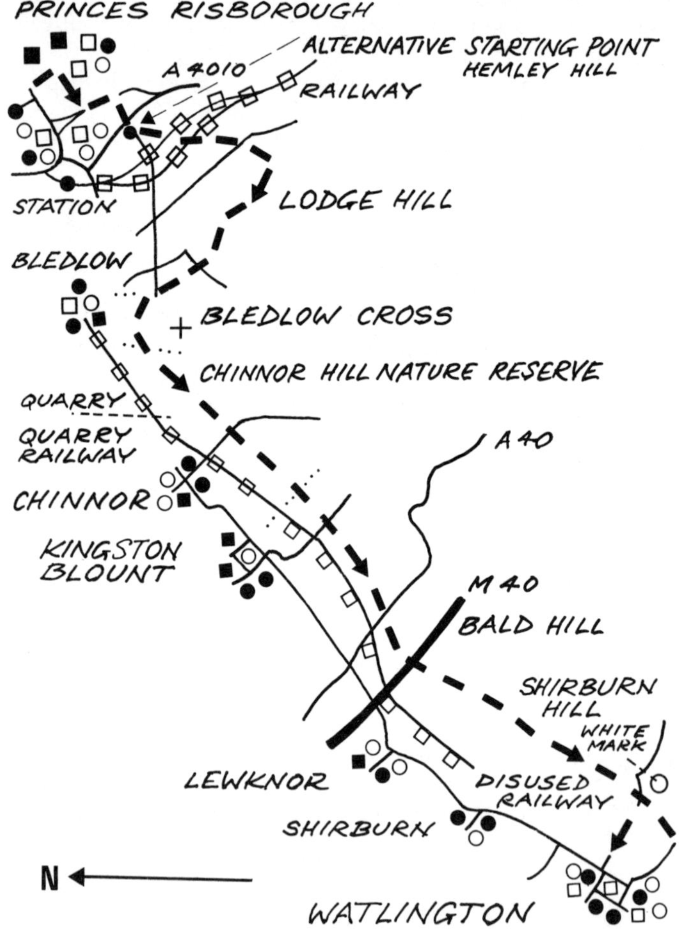

After meandering in the Risborough Gap and over Lodge Hill to Hempton Wainhill the path follows the Upper Icknield Way for 6 straight miles (9.5 km). This 'Upper' Way runs along the base of the escarpment, where there are fine views of the beech-clad slopes. Between Beacon Hill and Watlington the beech recedes and exposes the magnificent sweeping curves and embayments emphasized by Bald, Shirburn and Pyrton Hills. Other features along this stretch of the Path (with less pleasing associations) include Chinnor cement works and its quarries, through which we seem to walk on a tight-rope, the defunct section of the Princes Risborough–Watlington railway and the M40 motorway through Beacon Hill. If the walk proves too long and you decide to stop at Wainhill it will be a simple matter to descend to the lovely village of Bledlow.

For the sake of the purists we will start this section where we left off yesterday. But for those who would welcome a reduction in today's mileage I will see you later: 1 mile (1.6 km) further on at Hemley Hill (grid reference 803015) on the Upper Icknield Way, where there is a grass verge on which to park your car. (Whether or not you will get back to it at the end of the day is another matter!)

From Princes Risborough High Street turn into Horne Lane beside the White Lion public house and then right into New Road. Follow New Road uphill for ⅓ mile (0.5 km), where it becomes Brimmers Road, and turn right into the clearly marked Upper Icknield Way (**4**). Go along this until you meet a main road (A4010). Turn left here and, after ½ mile (0.8 km), turn right into a narrow road (the Upper Icknield Way again) signposted to Bledlow. In a short while you will arrive at a crossroad; go straight on here and, after passing a house on the left, leave the road and go into a field through a wide gap in the hedge on the left-hand side. This is grid reference 803015: the alternative starting point which was mentioned earlier.

Now follow the right-hand edge of the field for half its length and go half-left across the field approximately midway between two electricity pylons. The path may not be obvious but if you head for a white stile under telephone wires at the extremity of the field you cannot go far wrong. When you go over the stile you will soon realize that you are crossing a railway tunnel. There is another white stile a few yards further on, at the other side of the tunnel; go over this and turn slightly left and downhill, passing the left-hand side of some small trees, to a stile. After a few more yards you will come to another railway line. Cross the line to a stile and go along the left-hand side of a field for a few yards to another stile, then on through the next field to a stile in its far left-hand corner. There are small electricity pylons nearby. The stile leads you into a field; strike across this to a house at the centre of the field (it looks like a trespass, but it is not). Go round the house and follow the rough drive to a road; cross the road to a field opposite and follow its left-hand edge slightly uphill. Lodge Hill is directly ahead. Beyond a line of overhead electricity wires the field-edge bends left before resuming its upward direction. Follow this all the way up to the top left-hand corner of the field and go through a gap in the hedge to another field higher up. Go along the left-hand edge of this field and up to an open grassy area. The stile ahead of you is a convenient place to take a rest and contemplate the view back across the valley. On the summit of a distant ridge opposite you will see Lacey Green Windmill. This is being restored by the Chiltern Society with voluntary effort and will soon relive its former glory. Princes Risborough lies below the north-western extremity of the ridge, its church steeple clearly visible. Cut into the chalk on the hillside above the town is Whiteleaf Cross.

Having crossed the stile you should go half-right among scattered brambles across the slope of the hill. There are two stone plinths to guide you. Princes Risborough and Whiteleaf Cross will now be on your right. The path passes through a group of beech trees and out on to a grassy ridge. After a few hundred yards it descends the hill among scrub and small trees and then runs alongside a timber fence designed, so it seems, to keep you out of the adjacent field. In this field, on your right, are two Bronze Age bell barrows. They are just discernible as smoothly rounded mounds quite close to the fence. Excavation of these sites has revealed human bones, pottery fragments, finely worked flint saws and other flint implements. Follow the fence round as it passes between fields and go over a stile into the field on the left. Go across the field and over a crossing track to another stile and on again to a road.

Cross the road to a stile opposite and go along the left-hand border of a field. Go over a stile in the hedge a short distance before the field's far left-hand corner. Once over the stile you should keep more or less to the right-hand edge of the field for about ¼ mile (0.4 km), heading for the far right-hand extremity of a large beech wood (Bledlow Great Wood – much of it now felled and replanted). The exit from the field is at a stile close to an electricity power line.

The upper Icknield Way is on the other side of the stile. We shall be following this to Watlington and beyond; but if you have had enough by now a few steps forward along the Way and a right-turn down a hedge-lined track will lead you – after ½ mile (0.8 km) or so – into Bledlow village. (If you keep going you will discover a more interesting path later.) Bledlow is worth seeing in any case; it possesses a number of attractive cottages and a good pub – The Lions (which claims to be the only inn in Britain with plural lions). Alongside the church, but divided from it by a public footpath, there is a deep ravine, a geological accident quite atypical of the Chilterns. Through it flows the tiny River Lyde, the water emerging from the ground at a considerable depth.

Back on the Path the route for the keen lies straight ahead along the level trackway through the beech wood. You will soon pass a timber cottage on your right, and, ¼ mile (0.4 km) further on, a cottage on your left at a footpath 'junction'. The first of the two paths leading off to the right is the 'more interesting' route to Bledlow mentioned earlier. The path going uphill just beyond the cottage provides a rewarding diversion for those with an hour or so to spare, since it leads to Chinnor Hill Nature Reserve and to the Bledlow Cross. The reserve has the reputation of being an 'ecological close-up of the social history of the Earth's vegetative life', which to most of us means that it is a delightful place through which to walk and enjoy the natural world. It is the property of the Berkshire, Buckinghamshire and Oxfordshire Naturalists' Trust (BBONT) who have kindly allowed the public free access on foot.

Bledlow Cross is another of those mysterious hill figures cut into the chalk. It can be reached by going up the Nature Reserve path for about 200 yards (180 m) and scrambling up the very steep left bank at a point where the ground has been severely razed (by previous visitors). It is thought by some commentators that the Cross dates back to the Middle Ages. Others consider it to be no older than about three hundred years. Those are the dull facts (or fallacies!); on the lighter side a saying goes that if you run up and down and across it your strength will be renewed: a timely note for the faint-hearted.

Now back to the footpath 'junction'. The level track ahead passes a vegetable plot on the left-hand side before entering an area of scrub below Wainhill. As the scrub fades out a badly eroded section of the path fades in; it is rather unpleasant. The Chinnor road is soon crossed. Chinnor possesses some attractive houses and streets, but I will risk criticism by saying that there is little of interest to justify a diversion and that you will do well to continue on your way. After 1 mile (1.6 km) or so you cross the Kingston Blount road, where you will be accompanied by the disused track of the old Princes Risborough–Watlington railway. The line was opened in 1872 over its 8½ miles (13.5 kms) and was run by a small private company until

1883; it was then purchased for £23,000 by the Great Western Railway. The Princes Risborough–Chinnor section of the line serves the Chinnor cement works and remains in use.

Another mile (1.6 km) and you are at the A40 Stokenchurch–Oxford road (where accommodation is provided at Beacon Cottage). Go straight on from here and follow the track around the lower slope of Beacon Hill. The small beech wood on your right is Lewknor Copse; this is leased by BBONT from All Souls College in order to preserve the spurge laurel and the rare white and narrow-lipped helleborines. Aston Rowant Nature Reserve lies directly opposite Lewknor Copse. Quoting from the nature trail leaflet, 'The Reserve of approximately 300 acres was established in 1958 to conserve a fine example of chalk downland with a rich variety of plant life. It also provides a site for research into the methods of managing short turf on chalk.'

Now to the M40; a motorway anywhere in the Chilterns is bound to be a disaster, but especially so here. The impact of this incursion on the Chiltern skyline would have been lessened if the Minister of Transport of an earlier day had not flown in the face of all opposition in deciding on the present route. An alternative route, put forward by the two internationally respected experts Ove Årup and Geoffrey Jellicoe and all the amenity societies, was to have cut through woodland on the north-east side of the A40 with a less damaging effect on this beautiful stretch of downland. The motorway has inflicted irreparable damage to the Aston Rowant Nature Reserve through which it passes.

After suffering the indignity of a concrete M40 tunnel the Path crosses delightful open country below Bald Hill. (Bald indeed, but for a thin line of trees.) In summer the green carpet beneath your feet will be adorned with wild flowers: wild thyme, saxifrage, melilot, scabious, knapweed and many others. Now keep to the straight track for 2 miles (3.2 km) or so to the Watlington road (**5**). You will go under a lovely canopy of sycamore, oak and beech and over two crossing tracks. Turn right along the road for Watlington. To continue on the Path turn to (**6**) on page 47.

The pyramid-shaped White Mark cut into the chalk on Watlington Hill (best seen from lower down the road) has been likened to a 'ghostly shadow of a church spire lying along the hill'. It was cut in 1764 under the direction of Edward Horne of Greenfield. Why, I can only guess. You will find Watlington a delightful place, particularly when you explore the High Street beyond the confines of the seventeenth-century town hall (where the traffic seems to care little as it rips through the narrow streets). The High Street itself leads you to lesser streets and pathways where it is a pleasure to walk. Watlington can claim an important place in history in at least one respect: it was here that the anti-Royalist John Hampden spent the night before being fatally wounded at the Battle of Chalgrove Field on 18 June 1643. He died six days later.

Returning to Princes Risborough
Taxis: Venture Cars, telephone: Princes Risborough 6559; House's, telephone: Watlington 2319.

Staying in Watlington
The Well House, High Street, Watlington, telephone: Watlington 2025 and 2495.
Mrs Roberts, Cross Cottage, High Street, telephone: Watlington 2218.
Beacon Cottage (on Ridgeway Path), Kingston Blount, telephone: Kingston Blount 51219.

Eating in Watlington
Martha's Kitchen, Couching Street; The Well House, High Street; Barber's Cross Tea Room, High Street.

Chapter 5

WATLINGTON TO NUFFIELD

5 miles (8 km)

From Watlington – or rather ½ mile (0.8 km) south-east of Watlington – the Path follows the line of the Icknield Way as far as North Farm below Swyncombe Downs. Here it turns south towards Swyncombe itself: a secluded settlement seemingly untouched by the modern world. The Path continues in a southerly direction through Ewelme Park to the A423 road at Nuffield Common.

The Path is reached from Watlington by walking along the Watlington–Christmas Common road (Hill Road) for ½ mile (0.8 km) to where the Path crosses the road. Turn right on to the Path (**6**). After ½ mile (0.8 km) you will reach the B480 road. On the way you will have noticed Watlington Hill and Watlington Park. The house, which is just visible through a gap in the trees, is described by Nikolaus Pevsner as a 'neat Georgian brick box'. It was built in 1755 and had, until 1928, suffered numerous extensions and modifications. In 1954 it was 'reduced to its Georgian dimensions'. The hill is in the care of the National Trust and is part of a Site of Special Scientific Interest – the 'interest' being the ecology of the yew scrub.

Cross the road to the lane opposite and go along this for about ⅓ mile (0.5 km) until it meets a five-way junction just beyond a pond on the left. Keep straight on here (with two fine houses on your left) along a track which soon reduces to a narrow path between scrubby hedges. The path eventually comes out into the open and continues like this for a ¼ mile (0.4 km) before arriving at a road. Cross the road to the track opposite and go ahead (about 350 yards (320 m)) until you reach a farm track going off left between a line of trees and a farm building (North Farm). Turn on to this track (you are now leaving the Icknield Way) and go uphill for ⅓ mile (0.5 km) to the lower edge of a beech wood where the path divides into three ways. Take the right-hand branch which skirts the

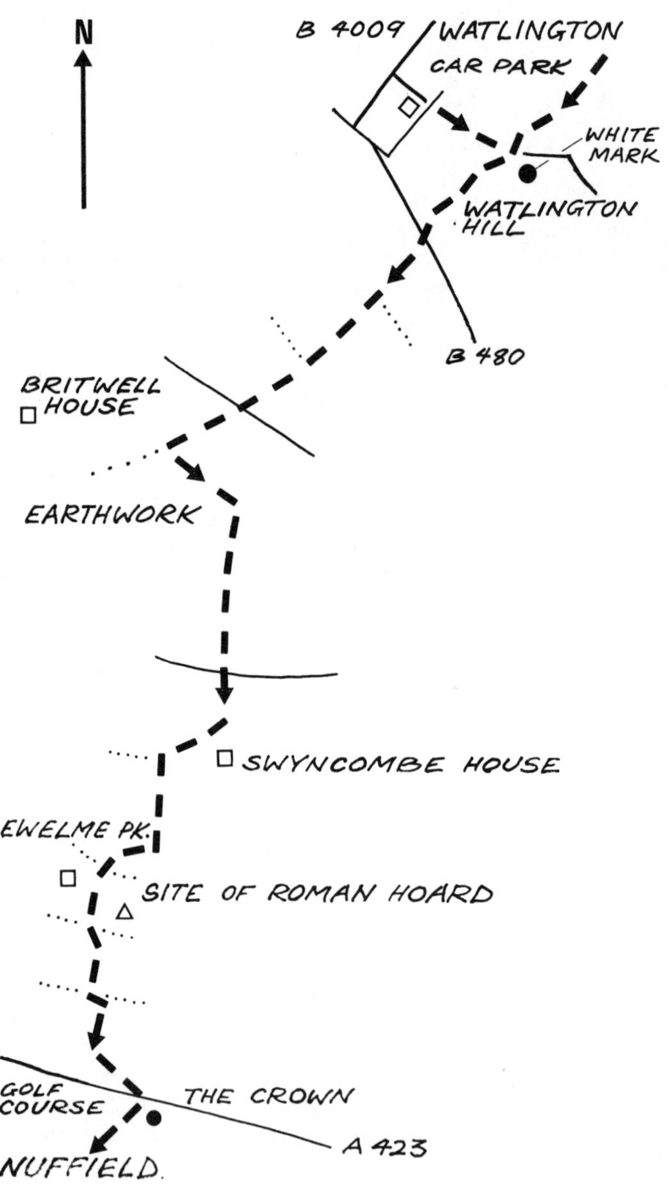
N
B 4009
WATLINGTON
CAR PARK
WHITE MARK
WATLINGTON HILL
B 480
BRITWELL HOUSE
EARTHWORK
SWYNCOMBE HOUSE
EWELME PK.
SITE OF ROMAN HOARD
GOLF COURSE
THE CROWN
A 423
NUFFIELD.

lower edge of the wood. Looking back you will see Britwell House in its attractive setting. The house was built in 1728 for Sir Edward Simeon, and is thought to have been designed by Edward Trubshawe. The wings were added in 1790, their top storeys in 1910. The previous owners, Mr David Hicks and Lady Pamela Hicks (daughter of the late Lord Mountbatten) had attempted to restore the house 'as near as possible to its original state'.

An extensive linear earthwork, largely hidden by a line of trees and scrub, reaches out westward from the foreground along the spur of Swyncombe Down. Because of its commanding position relative to the Icknield Way it seems likely that the earthwork had a military, perhaps defensive, role. Swyncombe Down itself is another of those Sites of Special Scientific Interest, noted for its chalk grassland flora.

Your path soon curves left and up into the wood and, just before levelling out, divides into two ways. Take the left-hand branch (the other leads into the open) and follow it up and then downhill to a path junction where prohibition signs abound. Carry straight on downhill into a dry valley beside some fine beech trees (which may soon be felled, I fear). Climb out of the valley along the right-hand edge of the large field to a road at the top. Go forward along the road to Swyncombe Church; Swyncombe House is just around the corner. Now do not go dashing on: this idyllic settlement is for unhurried contemplation. Notice in particular the beautifully carved faces and wings on the headstones in the churchyard. Swyncombe House, a 'thin and half-hearted attempt at the Jacobean style', was built in about 1840 to replace an earlier Elizabethan house that was destroyed by fire.

When you can tear yourself away go back to the corner and stand with the church at your left rear, and the new graveyard on your right. Go through the white gate directly ahead and along a track which gradually curves right. Ignore the first gate on the left and continue on further to a stile and gate on the left (about ¼ mile (0.4 km) from the iron gate near the church). Go over this and uphill – passing some isolated trees on your left – to another stile ahead at the entrance to a wood. Cross this stile and continue uphill through the wood along a path with a wire fence on the left. Beyond the next stile you will emerge at the corner of a field under some black poplar trees. Go forward along the left-hand edge of the field to its top left-hand corner and follow the top edge of the field. Ignore the stile in the fence and go through a gap in the corner of the field. Keep straight on along a farm track until you come to Ewelme Park Farm; turn left here and go between the farm buildings. Soon after crossing a drive you will pass the house itself. In 1953, on the occasion of the planting of a tree to commemorate Queen Elizabeth II's Coronation, a hoard of 202 Roman coins was unearthed about 300 yards (275 m) south of the house. This puts it somewhere in the paddock on your left. The hoard can be seen at the Ashmolean Museum in Oxford.

After a few hundred yards the path forks; take the left-hand branch. After about 30 yards (27 m) it forks yet again; take the right-hand branch and follow this between scrubby hedges for a few yards to a large field. Now you must launch out across this field with your sights aimed at the right-hand edge of a square plantation ½ mile (0.8 km) away. After crossing the field you will enter a long narrow wood. Go left in this and, after 100 yards (90 m), right into another field; again you must aim for the right-hand edge of the square plantation. Enter the plantation at its bottom right-hand corner and proceed uphill beside a wire fence for about 50 yards (45 m). Then go half-left through young trees to the top left-hand corner of the plantation. Here a gate leads you out on to Gangsdown Hill. Turn left in the road and go up to (or better still in to) The Crown public house.

Returning to Watlington

Bus 390 to Nettlebed (two-hourly, daily) then House's bus to Watlington (three-hourly, Monday–Saturday only).
Taxis: Jim's Taxis, telephone: Wallingford 37236; Hill's Taxis, telephone: Wallingford 37022.

Eating in Nuffield

The Crown public house.

Chapter 6

NUFFIELD TO GORING AND STREATLEY

9½ miles (15.25 km)

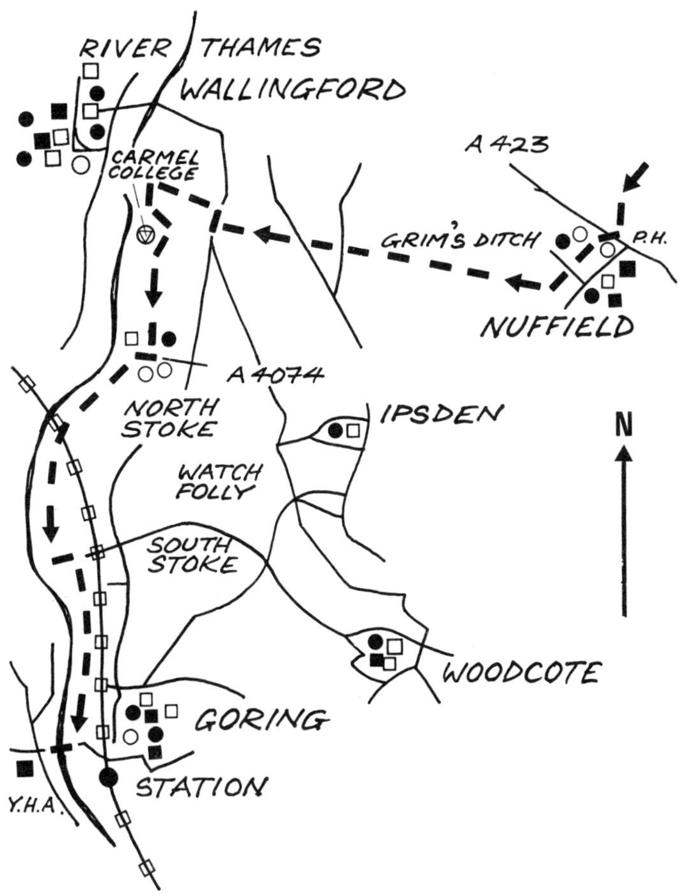

Now we come to the last few Chiltern miles; what better way to descend the escarpment than to follow the green line of Grim's Dyke as it drops from Nuffield to Mongewell Park and the Thames. From Mongewell Park the path strikes south-west through the lovely village of North Stoke and follows the east bank of the Thames to South Stoke; it then pursues a confined course between river and railway on its way down to Goring.

Leave the A423 road at Nuffield Common (grid reference 675877) along a rough drive starting from the right-hand side of The Crown public house. This takes you close to Fairway Cottage – so close that it feels like a trespass! Bear left round the cottage and follow the garden hedge to its end. You must then launch out across the golf course (at speed and keeping your head low!) to follow a line of white posts– each stencilled with a black acorn – all the way to the clubhouse. (The posts will have led you past a large hole on your left, and into a wooded area with waymarked trees.) Go over a stile on the right of the clubhouse and then across a field in the direction of Nuffield Church. Massingham's brief commentary on 'pepper-potted Nuffield Church' was that it had nothing in it and was kept locked on the principle of fastening the stable-door after the horse is stolen. That was in 1940; now you may enter freely.

About 100 yards (90m) beyond the church, where a flint wall ends, a stile leads into a field. From here, on a clear day, you will have a fine view across the Thames Valley to the Oxfordshire Plain; the scene is shared by the cooling towers at Didcot (almost mellowed by distance) and the Sinodun Hills, sometimes called the Wittenham Clumps, beyond Wallingford. Follow the top left-hand edge of the field until you reach its far left-hand corner. Go over a rail and straight ahead through trees for another 100 yards (90 m) to another rail. Continue to what you may soon realize is an arm of the enigmatic Grim's Dyke. Turn right here (not over the stile ahead).

Now begins a magnificent descent to the Thames Valley; few directions are necessary: simply follow the line of the dyke downhill for 3 miles (4.8 km) until you reach the entrance gate to Carmel College on the A4074 road. On your way down you

will cross two metalled roads – the first being the Icknield Way – and numerous cart tracks. The dyke becomes indistinct at times, fading out completely at one place. On your way down you will have a pleasant bird's-eye view of Wallingford through a break in the trees. It is interesting to compare the chalkiness of the dyke, as it crosses the plateau, with the brown of the fields on either side: it seems likely that the dyke-builders extracted their materials from distant chalky sites rather than spoil adjacent fertile land. Where the thorn scrub grows thinly along this green ribbon you may notice that many species of chalk-loving wild flowers have taken hold.

The path finally reaches the A4074 road immediately opposite the entrance to Carmel College. The college – a Jewish school – hides a greater name: Mongewell Park. It is a sad fact that the National Trust was prevented (because of legal difficulties) from accepting 'this lovely place by the Thames' with its late nineteenth-century mansion, its many acres of fine forest trees, and its ornamental lake. Now cross the A4074 road and go downhill for a few yards to a path on the left. This tree-shaded path is accompanied on its left-hand side by the college drive and the continuation of Grim's Dyke and leads to a branch of the drive (which in turn leads to a sports ground and new school buildings on the right). Cross this 'branch' to a path opposite and continue ahead under the trees until you reach a paved path, at which turn left. The path is bordered by a pasture on the left and takes you to a point alongside an inner entrance to the college. Keep straight on here, along a drive, passing some houses on the right. Behind the trees on your left is the 'ornamental lake' which was an attractive feature of the original estate. When the drive eventually turns right amongst scattered college buildings – with Mongewell Park House beyond – go straight ahead through a white gate and on to a path under tall trees. This will lead you to an iron gate in the perimeter fence of the park. Go through the gate and straight ahead along a path with a field left and a hedge right. The village of North Stoke is just ahead.

One of the first buildings encountered as you enter North Stoke is the beautifully restored Old Mill with the mill-stream (the Drincan) flowing beneath its walls. The Drincan runs down from a large pond behind Mill House; the pond is replenished by a spring. Following its centuries-old career in the grinding of corn and meal the Drincan was harnessed to drive a dynamo which supplied electricity to The Springs, the large house on the B4009. Parts of the dynamo can be seen beneath the Old Mill. To see the pond you should take the footpath almost opposite the village hall and walk the ¼ mile (0.4 km) to the B4009 road above. Dame Clara Butt, the celebrated singer, owned two houses in the village: Brook Lodge, the pink house in view from the bridge, and Prospect House, almost opposite the village hall. She is remembered for her remarkable contralto voice and for her part in the first performance of a number of Sir Edward Elgar's works – including 'Sea Pictures' in 1899 and 'Land of Hope and Glory' (from the 'Coronation Ode') in 1902.

Continue through the village and turn right at the T-junction (Church Lane) just before the farmyard of North-stoke Farm. This takes you alongside some cottages and to the church. Here you will find much of interest, including the fine old timbers of the entrance porch and chancel roof, the medieval wall paintings and the sundial on the south-facing wall. Dame Clara Butt died in 1936 and her grave, together with that of her husband and two young sons, is close to the west end of the church. 'With her whole heart she sang songs and loved Him that made her' is a tribute to a woman who experienced sorrow along with success: one of her sons died at the age of 19, the other at 28.

Go round the right-hand side of the church through the graveyard to a stile which leads you on to a lawn; then half-right across the lawn for a distance of 30 yards (27 m) to its far right-hand corner to follow a path with a timber fence right. This eventually leads you out into a field. Go along the right-hand edge of the field until you reach another stile, and yet again into another field leading to yet another stile. After crossing a stream you will see two concrete posts (a common feature hereabouts) with a gate opening on to a Thames-side meadow – an ideal place for your lunch-break!

After rest and refreshment return to the path by way of the concrete gateposts and continue in the same direction as before – along the right-hand edge of a field towards a stile at its far right-hand corner. Go past the right-hand side of a house to a T-junction, at which turn right; you will shortly arrive at a delightful place under chestnut trees on the river bank.

Now follow the left-hand bank of the Thames for 1¼ miles (2 km) across a succession of riverside meadows linked to each other by wooden gates. The path will lead you under the arches of Moulsford railway bridge. Built by the great nineteenth-century engineer Isambard Kingdom Brunel, the bridge, together with over 20½ miles (33 km) of the Great Western Railway from Reading to Steventon, was opened to the public on 1 June 1840. In 1893 it was doubled to its present width. The earlier span shows signs of decay but remains in service after more than 170 years' continuous use. Your 1¼ miles (2 km) finishes when you arrive at the busy boating centre at Moulsford. Here you must turn left into a rough track leading to South Stoke. Where the rough track ends at some cottages turn right into a tarred road and go ahead to a Y-junction. This is South Stoke, noted for its ancient farms, the oldest of which is Manor Farm just ahead of you. In the farmyard beyond the flint wall there is what is thought to be the second largest dovecot in the country (Yorkshire has the largest). It was built in the sixteenth century and houses about a thousand pigeon nests.

Take the right-hand branch of the Y-junction and, ignoring all turnings, keep ahead through the village. At the end of the village where the road turns left to go under a railway, keep straight on along a footpath signposted to Goring. The path runs across a field (from where you get a preview of the 'Berkshire' Downs) and passes a red-brick house on the left. The path changes to a track and later to a metalled road; houses proliferate and it becomes clear that you are in the suburbanized environs of Goring.

When the road turns left in hair-pin fashion to go *over* the railway keep straight on to join a path signposted to Goring; follow this path for ½ mile (0.8 km) as it runs first between iron fences and then as an unmetalled road, finally joining another road coming in from the left. Go forward to the summit of the road and join a path leaving the right-hand side opposite Clevemead housing estate. The path will take you right down into Goring. On your right as you cross the bridge is Goring Lock. Together with its neighbour at Cleeve ½ mile (0.8 km) upstream, the lock played an important part in Thames navigation when the commercial use of the river was more evident than it is today. It is here that a tragic accident took place in 1674: sixty people were drowned when the boat in which they were cruising capsized over the weir.

Goring Church should not be missed. Even if you are not versed in ecclesiastical matters you will agree that the unencumbered walls and the delicate tracery of the roof timbers endow this church with a beauty that is simple and refreshing. Hanging above the tower arch is an old bell which had been in use for more than 600 years – until 1929, when it was moved to its present position. To the left of the pulpit there is a memorial plaque engraved to the memory of Hugh Whistler who died on 17 January 1615 aged 216 years! While you contemplate this seemingly miraculous life-span I will sober your thoughts with the popular notion that the engraver was a little careless in his art.

Returning to Nuffield

Bus B from Sloane Hotel, Goring to Wallingford (two-hourly Monday–Saturday only; last bus 17.17). Then Bus 390 to Nuffield (two-hourly, daily).
Taxis: Jim's Taxis, telephone: Wallingford 37236; Hill's Taxis, telephone: Wallingford 37022.

Staying in Goring and Streatley

Leyland (bed and breakfast), 3 Wallingford Road, Goring, telephone: Goring 872119.
The John Barleycorn, Goring, telephone: Goring 872509.
Mrs Hudson, 18 Lockstile Way, Goring, telephone: Goring 873872.
Mrs Kemsley, Tumblegrove, Crays Pond, Goring, telephone: Goring 872346.
Streatley Youth Hostel (closed most Sundays), telephone: Goring 872278.

Bennets Wood Farm, Southridge, telephone: Goring 872377. (2 miles (3.2 km) from Streatley, bed and breakfast only).

Eating in Goring and Streatley
Goring: The John Barleycorn; Ye Miller of Mansfield.
Streatley: The Bull.

Chapter 7

GORING AND STREATLEY TO EAST ILSLEY

7 miles (11.25 km)

From Streatley the Path follows the near-straight line of the ancient Ridgeway westward along the 'Berkshire' Downs. The view across the vale is magnificent, but dominated for many miles by the massive cooling towers of Didcot power station and the sprawl of the Atomic Energy Research Establishment at Harwell. The distant Chiltern escarpment reaching out to the north-east is companion to the scene – a constant reminder of more pastoral aspects of the Ridgeway Path. Although it is within the capabilities of the average walker to complete the 15 miles (24 km) from Streatley to Wantage in one go, I have concluded this section at East Ilsley for the benefit of those who prefer a more leisurely day.

Before you set foot on the ancient highway a few minutes in St Mary's Church, Streatley and an hour or so on Loughdown Hill would be time well spent. On display in the church is an iron spear, a knife and a bronze buckle from the grave of a Saxon warrior excavated in 1932 on the site of a new bowling green. The remains were subsequently reburied in the churchyard. Loughdown Hill, which is in the care of the National Trust, overlooks Streatley from the north-west and offers fine views across the Thames to Goring and beyond.

From the main crossroads at the centre of Streatley (grid reference 592807) go north along the A329 road in the direction of Moulsford and Wallingford (a right turn if you have just crossed the Thames from Goring). In ¼ mile (0.4 km) the main road divides into the A417 and the A329: take the left-hand branch – the A417 – and go along this for ⅓ mile (0.5 km) to Rectory Road on the left. The entrance to Rectory Road is marked by a letter-box and a 'No Through Road' sign.

Go along Rectory Road for 1½ miles (2.4 km), passing Thurle Grange on your right, to Warren Farm. Although this stretch is part of the ancient Ridgeway, it is tarred all the way, but is very pleasant none the less. You will pass Warren Farm

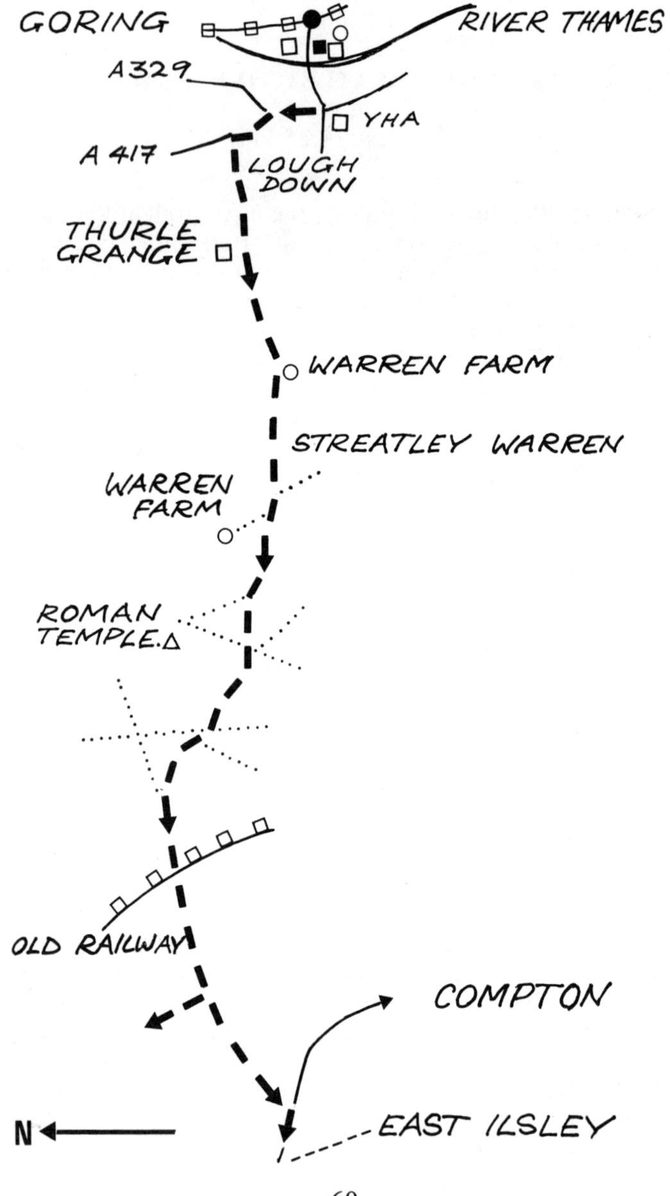
GORING
RIVER THAMES
A329
YHA
A 417
LOUGH DOWN
THURLE GRANGE
WARREN FARM
STREATLEY WARREN
WARREN FARM
ROMAN TEMPLE
OLD RAILWAY
COMPTON
N
EAST ILSLEY

cottages before arriving at the farm itself. A post-box stands beside the farm entrance; bear right here along the wide flint track. On your left is the impressive expanse of Streatley Warren. The track climbs gradually, and is tree-lined at first.

There is another Warren Farm at the top. *Do not* go down the farm drive but keep straight on. Avoid all paths going off to the right as you descend to a somewhat complicated junction ½ mile (0.8 km) from the summit. Where the junction is met by a path coming in from the left rear, take the left fork ahead; this passes the left-hand side of a group of hawthorn trees and meets a crossing track almost immediately. If you have time to spare, you could turn off right at the fork and walk ½ mile (0.8 km) to the site of a fourth-century Roman encampment on Lowbury Hill. A great quantity of Roman pots, as well as bricks, tiles, coins and oyster shells, has been found in and around the encampment. A Saxon burial mound stands nearby. Apparently, a female skeleton with its skull smashed in was found buried in the foundations of a stone wall.

If this grim detail has set you against the diversion, you should go straight on for ½ mile (0.8 km) to another track junction. Keep straight on here, going over two crossing tracks within 50 yards (45 m) of each other. You will pass a wood on your right almost immediately and, in ¼ mile (0.4 km), a small copse of conifer trees, also on your right. A little further on the track cuts deeply into the chalk just before a Y-junction. Fork left here along a double track. The Ridgeway Path has taken leave of the true Ridgeway for the time being and follows the Roman Fair Mile across Compton Downs.

The track ahead crosses a bridge over a disused railway. This is a relic of the Didcot, Newbury and Southampton Joint Railway which was incorporated in 1873 to cross the Berkshire and Hampshire Downs. The Didcot–Newbury section – the Berkshire Downs part – was opened in 1882. The promoters' dream of a trunk route carrying a heavy volume of traffic to and from Southampton was not realized, due largely to the lack of interest on the part of the operating company, the GWR. It was a commercial failure and a disaster for the shareholders. But the line did have one moment of glory, for it is said that during the twelve months prior to D-Day (6 June

1944) about 16,000 military trains rode the metals to Southampton. The platform at Churn Halt is in view about ¼ mile (0.4 km) to the north.

Follow the well-worn track uphill, ignoring the right-hand fork about 300 yards (275 m) beyond the railway bridge. After an uphill, straight ½ mile (0.8 km) followed by a short downhill stretch you will meet a concrete crossing road, where you should turn right if you are going on to Wantage (**7**). To continue on the Path turn to (**8**) on page 65.

If East Ilsley is your destination you should cross the drive and go ahead for ¾ mile (1.2 km) to a road. Turn right there for East Ilsley. As declared on an inscribed stone standing but a few score yards from the centre of the village, East Ilsley was an important trading centre from the thirteenth century onwards. Great sheep fairs were held which were second only in importance to Smithfield. Also close to the village centre stands East Ilsley Hall which, in the words of Nikolaus Pevsner is 'quite a swagger early Georgian House'. It is accompanied by Kennet House opposite.

Returning to Goring and Streatley

Bus 112 to Rowstock Corner (two-hourly Monday–Saturday only, until 15.15) then Bus 302/304 to Didcot (hourly Monday–Saturday), then train to Goring (hourly Monday–Saturday).

Taxis: Harrold's Taxis, telephone: Didcot 814321; Bob's Radio Cabs, telephone: Didcot 814679.

Staying in East Ilsley and Compton

Swan Hotel, East Ilsley, telephone: East Ilsley 238.

The Swan, Compton, telephone: Compton 269.

Mrs Jarret, The Forge House, Compton, telephone: Compton 387.

Chapter 8

EAST ILSLEY TO WANTAGE

11 miles (17.75 km)

You may well object to setting out from East Ilsley in what appears to be the wrong direction. This apparent aberration on my part is in order that you may join the Ridgeway Path at the point that marked the end of yesterday's walk, with the added bonus of a fine view from Several Down.

From East Ilsley go along the Compton road for ½ mile (0.8 km) to a wide track on the left immediately beyond a private drive to an Agricultural Research Council property (grid reference 499812). The track runs between hedge and field and crosses two lesser tracks before reaching a concrete drive (about ¾ mile (1.2 km) along from the Compton road). Turn left here and, after a few hundred yards go past what is another entrance to the Agricultural Research Council property. This

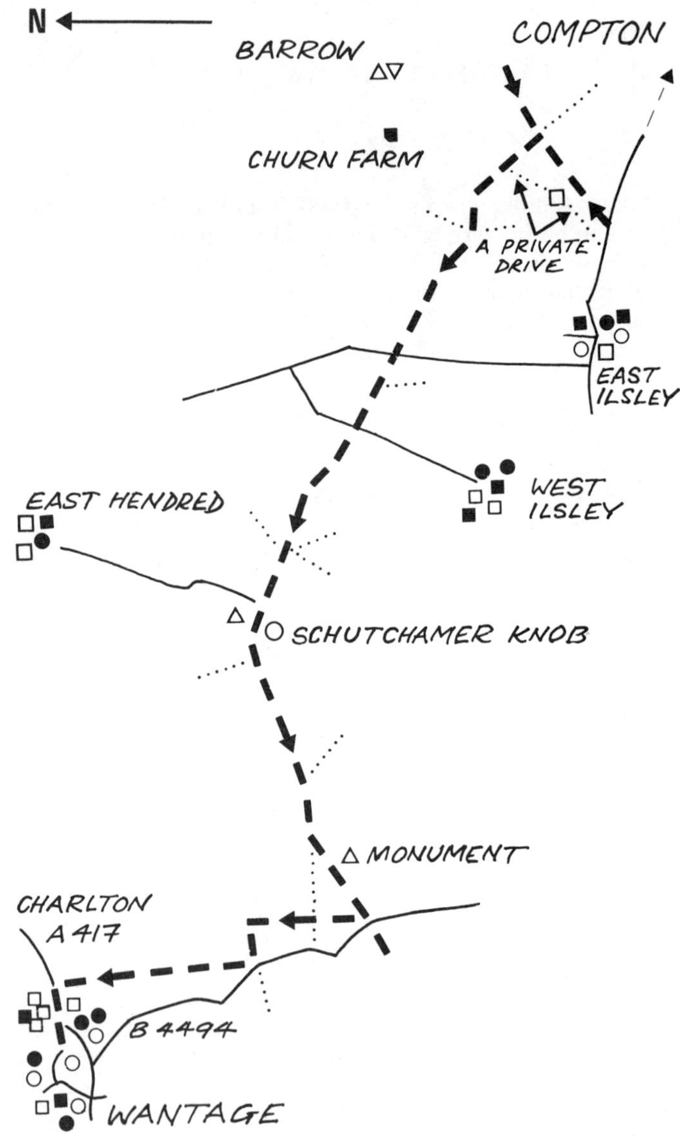
N
COMPTON
BARROW
CHURN FARM
A PRIVATE DRIVE
EAST ILSLEY
WEST ILSLEY
EAST HENDRED
SCHUTCHAMER KNOB
MONUMENT
CHARLTON
A 417
B 4494
WANTAGE

is where the stalwarts who are walking all the way from Streatley to Wantage in one day will join in (**8**).

One mile (1.6 km) to the north-east, in the general direction of the tree-capped top of Churn Hill, you will see Churn Farm. On the slope behind the farm is the site of a Bronze Age barrow cemetery, and, in the fields below, you have a glimpse of the disused railway track that we crossed earlier (page 61). The concrete drive gives way to a grassy track. The track soon curves left and then right before going uphill alongside a horse gallop over Several Down. On a clear day you will see the distant escarpment of the Chiltern hills, punctuated by the monument on Coombe Hill, Wendover, and the plume of smoke from the Chinnor cement works.

A quarter of a mile (0.4 km) down from the summit of Several Down the path meets a sandy bridleway. Go over this and proceed to the A34 road. Cross the A34 to the track opposite and go along this for almost a mile (1.6 km) to a by-road (this leads to the pretty village of West Ilsley, 1 mile (1.6 km) south). Cross the by-road and continue ahead for 1½ miles (2.4 km) to the point where a road (from East Hendred) terminates. Situated in the wood on the left (about half-way along) there is what was once a very large mound called Scutchamer Knob. The mound, which is mentioned in the Saxon Chronicles of AD 1006 was severely mutilated by nineteenth-century archaeologists; its height was originally 77 feet (23 m) but is now little more than a shell with walls a few feet high. Included among the insignificant 'finds' were fragments of Iron Age pottery, an iron buckle and a large charred oak post, but no interment. The shell is largely obscured by a dense covering of trees and is best seen in winter when the leaves have fallen.

Continuing ahead along the Ridgeway you will soon pass an Ordnance Survey plinth on your right. One mile (1.6 km) further on you will pass a wood on your right, and lesser woods at intervals thereafter up to the point where the path divides into two ways. Bear left along the grassy uphill path leading to a monument. The monument, standing on what may have been an Iron Age burial mound, was erected in memory of Colonel Sir Robert James Loyd-Linsey, Baron Wantage of Lockinge, V.C., K.C.B., who died in 1901. For those who are none the wiser, I quote from *Wantage, Past and Present* (by A. Gibbons and E. C. Davey, 1901): 'It is impossible within the limits of this notice to give any adequate idea of the fullness of Lord Wantage's life, or the great extent of the useful, patriotic and philanthropic labours in which he was engaged up to almost the moment of his death.' He was a 'driving force' in the early days of the Didcot, Newbury and Southampton Joint Railway (we crossed its disused track on yesterday's walk), a distinguished soldier of the Crimean War, and one of the first recipients of the Victoria Cross. His prominent position on the Downs is well-earned!

In about ½ mile (0.8 km) you will arrive at the B4494 Wantage road (**9**). Turn to (**10**) on page 75 if you are continuing on the Path. To terminate your day in Wantage you have now to choose between almost certain injury along this pavement-less road and a safe journey along a track which runs roughly parallel to it. To get on to this track go through a gate about 50 yards (45 m) before the junction of the Ridgeway Path with the road; this leads into a steeply sloping field at the lowest corner of which is another gate. Go through this gate and on to a path which runs alongside a horse gallop. Turn left 100 yards (90 m) after passing a small plantation. This takes you back to the B4494. Turn right here and follow the long, straight, tiresome track (*not* the B4494) to Charlton on the A417. Turn left here for Wantage.

If your bus is not due for an hour or so, the time may be pleasantly spent in one of the town's refreshment houses and in viewing the Market Square. The individual buildings are not spectacular in themselves but the total effect is warm and homely. Here, as elsewhere, such simple qualities are not enough to prevent the encroachment of the developer, so enjoy it while you may. Alfred the Great's statue stands at one end of the square; it was given to the town by Lord Wantage. To the south of the square, in Portway, the Wantage Museum holds an interesting collection of exhibits relating to the history and archaeology of the Vale of the White Horse and the town itself.

Wantage is of particular importance to the tram enthusiast: it was the first town in England to operate a steam-powered tram service. This was inaugurated on 1 August 1876 and ran from the town to Wantage Road Station (on the Great Western Railway), a distance of 2½ miles (4 km). Passenger services ceased in 1925, freight in 1945. One of the original steam locomotives (No. 5, Shannon) was preserved for a time at Wantage Road Station but later (1969) moved to the Great Western Society depot at Didcot. Built in 1857, she is probably the oldest working steam locomotive in existence.

Returning to East Ilsley

Bus 302/304 to Rowstock Corner (hourly Monday–Saturday; three-hourly Sunday), then Bus 112 to East Ilsley (two-hourly until 15.33, Monday–Saturday only).
Taxis: Robert's Taxis, telephone: Wantage 3503.

Staying in Wantage

Maindy Lodge (bed and breakfast), Charlton Road, telephone: Wantage 2813.
Royal Oak Inn, Newbury Street, telephone: Wantage 3129.
The Bear Hotel, Market Square, telephone: Wantage 3781.

Eating in Wantage

Chatterbox, Newbury Street; Epicure Restaurant, Grove Street; M & A, Newbury Street.

Chapter 9

WANTAGE TO BISHOPSTONE

13 miles (21 km)

But for the magnificent panorama that enshrines the bare sweep of Hackpen Hill, today's walk is through landscape similar in appearance to more easterly aspects of the Downs. Most notable of the man-made features along this stretch of the Ridgeway are Iron Age Segsbury Camp, Uffington Castle, the White Horse of Uffington and the Wayland's Smithy long barrow. From Blowingstone Hill westward the Ridgeway is accompanied at close range by a chain of villages straddled along the foot of the Downs: Kingston Lisle, Woolstone, Compton Beauchamp, Ashbury, Idstone, Bishopstone. Bishopstone is without question the most beautiful and it is appropriate that today's walk should end there. If your feet can stand the strain there is much pleasure to be had from walking the return journey to Wantage through these lovely villages.

For those who will not be deflected from doing every inch of the Ridgeway Path there is little choice but to walk the final part (that long dusty track) of yesterday's excursion in reverse, and I must apologize to these hearty stalwarts for relegating such details to the end of the chapter. For the benefit of those with moderate inclinations I will describe a very pleasant link with the Downs that takes in the village of Letcombe Regis and connects to the Ridgeway at Segsbury Camp.

A narrow metalled path leaves the B4507 (Portway) opposite Priory Road just a short distance beyond the new Recreation Centre. The Civic Hall car park and King Alfred's School are close by. You simply follow this path all the way to Letcombe Regis, alongside playing fields and Letcombe Brook and into a road running through the centre of a small housing estate. Go straight over the crossroad at the other end of the estate (there is a telephone box here) and follow the road round through the village as far as the church. According to one commentator, the church was 'severely manhandled' in

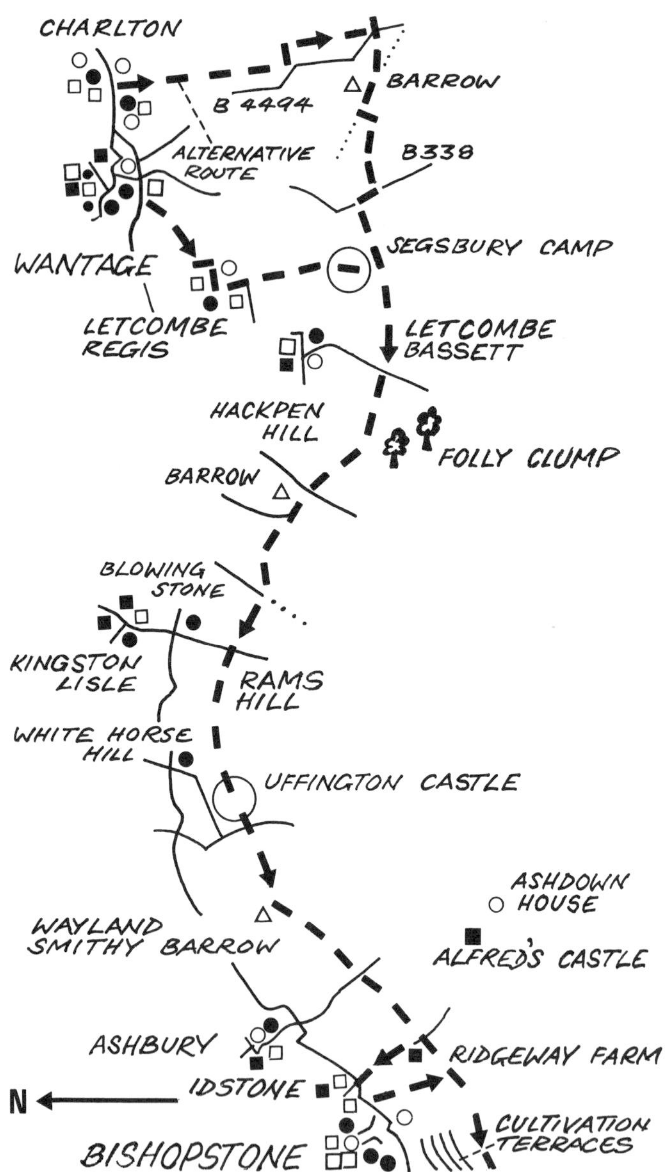
CHARLTON
BARROW
B 4494
ALTERNATIVE ROUTE
B338
WANTAGE
SEGSBURY CAMP
LETCOMBE REGIS
LETCOMBE BASSETT
HACKPEN HILL
FOLLY CLUMP
BARROW
BLOWING STONE
KINGSTON LISLE
RAMS HILL
WHITE HORSE HILL
UFFINGTON CASTLE
ASHDOWN HOUSE
WAYLAND SMITHY BARROW
ALFRED'S CASTLE
ASHBURY
RIDGEWAY FARM
N
IDSTONE
CULTIVATION TERRACES
BISHOPSTONE

1863. You may wish to break off at this point and make up your own mind on the matter.

With the assumption that you have not crossed over to the church you should now turn left at the road junction and continue through the village to a left-hand turn. There is a signpost here proclaiming 'Ridgeway 1¼ miles'. *Do not go* down there for you will miss Segsbury Camp and even more of the Ridgeway, but follow the road first left and then right and uphill for 1 mile (1.6 km) to the camp. Although Iron Age in origin, Segsbury Camp – otherwise known as Letcombe Castle – was modified in Saxon times. In 1871 fragments of human bones, pieces of pottery, and flint scrapers were found in a flint cist beneath a sarsen stone in the rampart of the camp. The route through the centre of the camp leads directly to the Ridgeway, where you should turn right. This is the point of arrival for those who have come up to the Ridgeway from Charlton (**11**).

The Ridgeway now climbs gently to the summit of Rats Hill where you get a view of Hackpen Hill, Wantage and Letcombe Regis. From here the track drops steeply down to Letcombe Bassett, some ½ mile (0.8 km) away in the lee of the Downs (for your interest only). Continuing ahead you will, after ½ mile (0.8 km), cross the road above Gramp's Hill (another steep drop down to Letcombe Bassett). Onward a few yards and we have a dramatic transition from the hedged track which has been such a familiar feature of the Ridgeway so far; and with massive Hackpen Hill in pride of place. A summit of the path is reached soon after passing the weather-worn copse of beech trees called Folly Clump. If your eyesight is keen (or if you are sensible enough to carry a pair of binoculars) you will just make out a small burial mound on Hackpen Hill above the head of a coombe called Devil's Punchbowl.

In less than 1 mile (1.6 km) you will arrive at the B4001 road (signposted to Sparsholt). Cross this to the tarred road opposite. The mound in a field immediately to your right is a bowl barrow. This was excavated by Greenwell in the nineteenth century, and an 'unaccompanied primary cremation' found. About 100 yards (90 m) beyond the B4001 you must leave the metalled road by turning half-left; after ½ mile (0.8 km) the path curves left and slopes downhill to a crossing track. Before descending you may care to spot the villages of Kingston Lisle, Sparsholt and Childrey at the foot of the Downs. Directly ahead of you at a distance of 2 miles (3.2 km) is Whitehorse Hill – 856 feet (261 m) high.

After the crossing track the Ridgeway goes over a hill to meet the Kingston Lisle road above Blowingstone Hill. The piece of sarsen stone known as The Blowingstone and immortalized in *Tom Brown's Schooldays* stands beside a cottage garden at the bottom of Blowingstone Hill. It has a hole through which, it is said, can be blown a low-pitched wailing note. Legend has it that the stone was used by King Alfred as a trumpet to call his soldiers together. The cottage has less reputable associations: it was once the Blowingstone Inn but lost its licence long ago for being a haunt of poachers.

Your next landmark is Whitehorse Hill 1½ miles (2.4 km) from the Kingston Lisle road. The hill is capped by the extensive ramparts of Iron Age Uffington Castle, access to which is through a gate in a wire fence on the right-hand side of the Ridgeway. Over the brow of the hill on the north-facing slope is the magnificent White Horse of Uffington, carved out of the downland turf. The age and original purpose of this chalk monument are controversial, but it seems likely that it was first cut by Iron Age man, in view of its similarity to the figures that appear on coins of that period and the close proximity of an Iron Age fort. The cleaning up of the Horse (the 'scouring') was an important part of the open-air festivals that took place on the hill at intervals of seven years or so until 1857. These were great occasions for games, competitions, dancing, singing and drinking. It was reported that 30,000 people attended the festival in the year 1780! A local saying tells us that 'while men sleep, the Horse climbs up the Hill'. This is not as outrageous as it sounds, for as the soil falls away from the upper edges and exposes more of the chalk, and the lower edges silt up and become colonized by grass, so the horse does indeed climb the hill. Beneath you on the downland side of the Icknield Way is the flat-topped knob of Dragon Hill where St George is reputed to have killed the Dragon. The bare patch is where its blood poured out.

Back on the Ridgeway you will soon pass a stile in the fence on your right. (This – for your interest only – is the way to the car park and ice-cream van.) The Ridgeway continues straight ahead, down through an avenue of hawthorn bushes and over two crossing tracks. About ⅓ mile (0.5 km) on from the last crossing, and just off the Ridgeway, is Wayland's Smithy long barrow. The site was excavated 1962–3 and found to consist of one burial chamber overlaid by another. Both have been dated at about the middle of the Neolithic period (New Stone Age). The excellent state of 'preservation' of the barrow is largely due to its reconstruction in 1964. The legend of Wayland the Smith was that he made 'swords none could resist and winged armour that carried one over the land like an eagle'. He would shoe a traveller's horse if a penny was left on one of the stones.

A crossing track is soon reached and ¾ mile (1.2 km) further on is the Lambourn–Ashbury road. If you now look in a southerly direction (half-left with respect to the Ridgeway ahead) in line with the right-hand edge of a large wood you will see (binoculars assumed) the green mound of Alfred's Castle about 1½ miles (2.4 km) away. This small Iron Age camp was robbed of much of its stone work during the building of Ashdown Park, a country house nearby, in the garden of which the camp stands. You will have a distant view of Ashdown Park later on from the slope of Charlbury Hill.

Half a mile (0.8 km) ahead the Ridgeway crosses a farm track by some barns and, after a further ¾ mile (1.2 km), it meets Ridgeway Farm on the Bishopstone road. Turn right here and go down to Bishopstone (**12**). To continue on the

Path turn to (**13**) on page 78.

You will not need me to extol the exceptional beauty of this downland village, with its thatched and whitewashed cottages 'enchantingly hidden and devious among gardens' and the mill-pond fed from the crystal clear waters of a stream. Alfred Williams, in his book *Villages of the White Horse* (published in 1913), gives an interesting account of day-to-day life in Bishopstone. Of two of the village industries, he wrote 'almost every day the huge wheel of the mill revolves under the weight of the foaming water, and rumbles beneath the high wall. The school, the blacksmith's shop, and the mill are all close together, the children are happy in their situation, and in the opportunities they have for viewing the several industries; they throng around the smithy door, and peer over at the mighty wheel each time they pass along, delighted to see the gleaming waters leaping down, and to view the merry fizzing sparks shooting out underneath the stroke of the blacksmith's hammer.' The parish church is a fine building in an attractive setting. Inside there is an interesting font, fragments of medieval coloured glass, and a thought-provoking epitaph – a sermon in stone to Charles Curtis who escaped shipwreck in 1822. In Alfred Williams's day a curfew bell was rung every night from eight till nine during the foggy months as a guide for those who might be lost on the Downs.

Wantage to the Ridgeway: Alternative Route

At the eastern end of Wantage at Charlton, Lark Hill runs up from the A417 road just beyond the Lord Nelson public house. From the top of Lark Hill a long, straight track runs south for 1½ miles (2.4 km) or so. Where this meets the B4494 road you should turn left into a path. Go along this for ¼ mile (0.4 km) and turn right at a crossing path; you will pass a small group of young trees on your right and a horse gallop on your left. Ahead a gate leads into a steeply sloping field; in the top right-hand corner of the field another gate leads on to the Ridgeway. Cross the B4494 Wantage road to the track opposite (**10**). After 200 yards (180 m) the track turns left; *do not* turn left with it but go straight ahead along the wide grassy sward. About ½ mile (0.8 km) further on (where you are met by another track coming in from the left rear) there is a grass-covered tumulus immediately to the right of the path. A bronze awl and a bronze riveted dagger were found here when the tumulus was excavated in 1938.

After another ½ mile (0.8 km) you must turn into what soon becomes a metalled farm track immediately beyond a small group of trees. In case of doubt there are other features marking this point: a farmhouse and a ruined cottage – with a copse beyond it – stand about 200 yards (180 m) to the right (north) and a track comes in from the left rear. The farm track soon turns right and takes you past Whitehouse Farm and on to the A338 Wantage–Hungerford road. Turn right along the A338 and in about 200 yards (180 m) – just before a house on the left – turn left along a stony track. After ½ mile (0.8 km) you will see the rampart of Segsbury Camp. You can get a closer look and enjoy a stroll along the rampart by turning right at a farm crossing ahead. The walk continues at (**11**) on page 71.

Returning to Wantage

Bus 475 to Woolstone (Saturday 16.48) then taxi: Robert's Taxis, telephone: Wantage 3503.

Eating in Bishopstone

The True Heart, telephone: Wanborough 462.

Staying and Eating in Ashbury

The Rose and Crown, telephone: Ashbury 222.

Chapter 10

BISHOPSTONE TO OGBOURNE ST GEORGE

9½ miles (15.25 km)

Today you will see the last of that landscape so characteristic of the downland ridge from Streatley westward; a landscape of extensive views often held in check by hedgerows and trees and by the vicissitudes of the Path itself. You will have constant reminders of the works of man, both ancient and modern: the age-old cultivation terraces above Bishopstone; the M4 motorway slipping almost unobtrusively through the Downs; the Iron Age encampment on Liddington Hill; and the great urban sprawl of Swindon a few miles north-west.

Go along the path that runs between Bishopstone's village school and the community centre and enters the delightful precinct of ancient cottages (which I trust you will have fully explored before setting out on today's walk) tucked away behind the mill-pond. You should ignore paths going off to the left and right and go ahead into the narrow path close to the left-hand wall of Lynden Cottage. You will eventually reach a drive; turn right on to this and stay with it as it evolves into a footpath. The stream that has accompanied you from Bishopstone suddenly comes to an end in a gorge bedded with watercress. 'Suddenly starts' would be more accurate, since it is here that the water breaks out of the ground.

The path ends at a kissing-gate and leads you into a field. Go up to the top right-hand corner of the field and join a trackway at a stile and gate. Where the trackway terminates you have about the best view possible – whilst remaining on the right side of the law of trespass – of the cultivation terraces. At close range they are very impressive indeed: giant-size steps cut into the hillside. While the purpose of these terraces is quite clear – that of growing crops on level ground under the protection of the hillside – their age can only be guessed at. Medieval, Saxon, Bronze Age are three proposals; and that does not leave much; to me a very early period – the Bronze Age perhaps – seems the most likely. The site was ideally situated

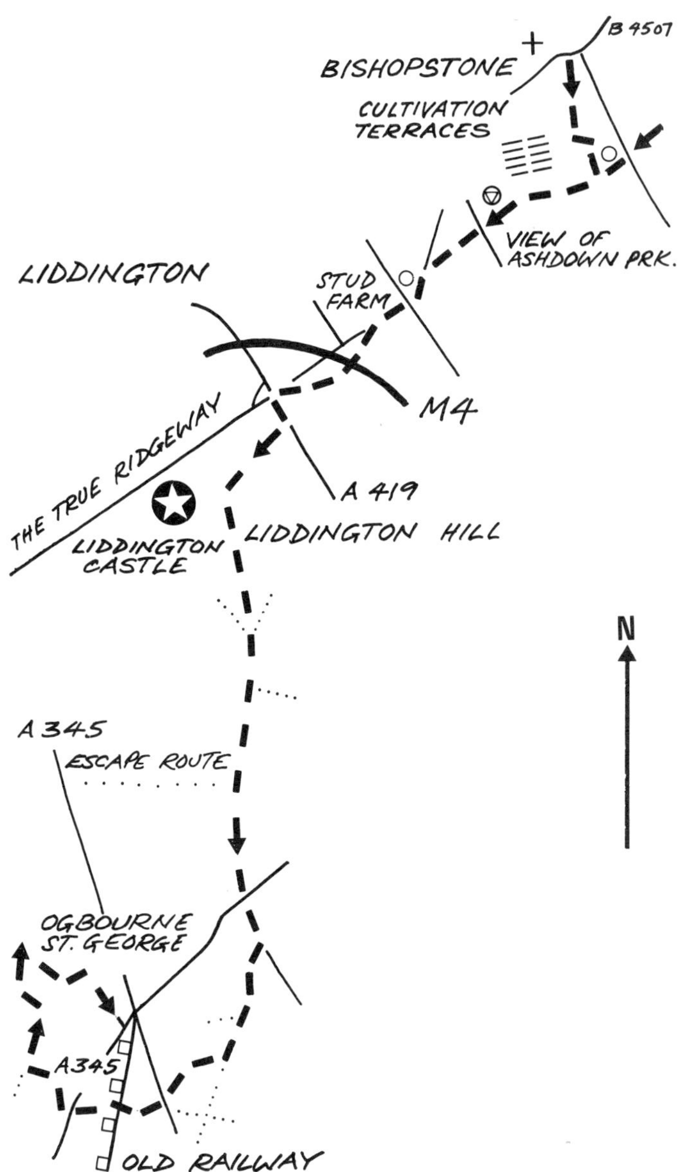
B 4507
BISHOPSTONE
CULTIVATION
TERRACES
VIEW OF
ASHDOWN PRK.
LIDDINGTON
STUD
FARM
M4
THE TRUE RIDGEWAY
A 419
LIDDINGTON
CASTLE
LIDDINGTON HILL
N
A 345
ESCAPE ROUTE
OGBOURNE
ST. GEORGE
A345
OLD RAILWAY

below the ridge-top but well above the uninhabitable vale: a compromise that would have become increasingly inessential as time progressed.

Now go through the gap in the fence on the left and proceed half-left into a wide valley. Follow this up as it bears right and narrows into a coombe. At the top of the coombe a gate leads you on to the Ridgeway. Turn right and go uphill (**13**).

Ashdown House can soon be seen about 2 miles (3.2 km) eastward. The house was built in 1665 for Elisabeth of Bohemia, sister of Charles I, by her admirer the first Lord Craven. 'A perfect doll's house' is Nikolaus Pevsner's apt description of this neat four-storeyed house with cupola and golden ball. Part of the interior of the house was given to the National Trust in 1956.

After ½ mile (0.8 km) or so you will cross the south-eastern flank of Charlbury Hill, on the top of which is an Ordnance Survey plinth. Another ½ mile (0.8 km) further the Ridgeway is joined by a road coming in from the right. Go ahead along this to a crossroad by The Shepherds' Rest – the only pub on the Ridgeway and a halting place of shepherds and drovers in times past. Cross to the road opposite and continue straight ahead, with the grounds of a stud farm (King Edward's Place) on your right.

After crossing the M4 motorway the road meets the A419 Aldbourne–Swindon road. (There is a barn and a bus-stop here.) Turn left along the A419 and, after 300 yards (275 m), right along an uphill track towards Liddington Hill. You have now broken loose from the Ridgeway proper, which strikes its low-lying course direct to Hackpen Hill on the Marlborough Downs. The small clump of beech trees ahead does not mark the summit of Liddington Hill; this is ½ mile (0.8 km) further on. There is, however, a good view from the far side of the clump which is well worth the short diversion. The track levels out now and appears to be heading for the ramparts of Iron Age Liddington Castle on the top of the Hill directly ahead. I say 'appears' because it gets tantalizingly close but curves away to the left without making contact. It is unfortunate that no right of way exists between the Ridgeway and the castle.

The road immediately below the hill to the north is the route of the true Ridgeway. It is from here that the castle can best be approached, but not without a fairly stiff climb. The hill is often referred to as Richard Jefferies' 'Mount of Meditation' on account of the many excursions this nineteenth-century essayist is reputed to have made to the hill. The following extract from his little book *The Story of my Heart* adequately portrays his feelings. 'There was a hill to which I used to resort at such periods. The labour of walking three miles to it, all the while gradually ascending, seemed to clear my blood of the heaviness accumulated at home. On a warm summer day the slow continued rise required continual effort, which carried away the sense of oppression. The familiar everyday scene was soon out of sight, I came to other trees, meadows and fields; I began to breathe a new air and to have a fresher aspiration . . . moving up to the sweet, short turf, at every step my heart seemed to obtain a wider horizon of feeling; with every inhalation of the rich, pure air, a deeper desire. The very light of the sun was whiter and more brilliant here.'

The Ordnance Survey plinth on the ramparts of the castle has a plaque engraved in honour of Richard Jefferies and Alfred Williams. Alfred Williams's book, *Villages of the White Horse,* makes good reading for Ridgeway walkers. Jefferies' birthplace, Coate Farm, is some 3 miles (4.8 km) away on this side of Swindon. It houses a small museum open on certain days of the week.

After the Path passes its point of nearest approach to the castle it curves left to a gate and follows a hawthorn hedge before breaking out into open country. Barbury Castle, that other Iron Age hill-fort through which we will pass on tomorrow's walk, is now at a distance of 5 miles (8 km) to the south-west (half-right if you are facing the Path ahead). The Path now follows the left-hand edge of two large fields in succession; then an iron gate leads you alongside a small field. Near the far end of the field bear right to meet a crossing track. Go over this and straight ahead, first to the right of a small wood and then into a hedge-lined track. There is another crossing track ½ mile (0.8 km) further on, which, if you feel like throwing in the sponge, will take you down to the A345 and the Swindon bus (route 470 from Chiseldon Camp). At this point it is worth noting that I have concluded today's walk at the far side of Ogbourne St George in order to reduce

tomorrow's mileage, so do not lose heart if you seem to be forever heading in the wrong direction. There are numerous short-cuts down to Ogbourne hereafter and you need not stay the course to the bitter end.

After emerging from the hedge-lined track you will cross a large field, with a wire fence immediately to your right. This will set you down on the Aldbourne–Ogbourne road. Cross to the road opposite, signposted 'Chase Woods Farm'. Go along this for ¼ mile (0.4 km) to the 'start' of a wood (on the left) and turn off the road half-right along a rough track. You now have ¾ mile (1.2 km) of path running almost straight and level to a crossing track beside an unidentifiable brick-built structure (you must be careful *not* to turn right half-way along this stretch, down a somewhat overgrown path beside a cattle trough). Turn right at the crossing and follow the track as it bends left and runs downhill to a road beside a new house. Cross over to the path opposite (not the wide track in the adjacent field) and follow this down to the A345 road by some thatched cottages. You will go under a decapitated railway bridge on the way down. This line was once an important north–south link between the Great Western Railway at Swindon and the London and South Western Railway at Andover. The Swindon–Marlborough section was opened in 1881.

Cross over the A345 to the road displaying a 'No Through Road' sign. This road meanders through an attractive cottage settlement and, after crossing the river Og, evolves into a stony track. There is a T-junction ahead, where you should turn right and go along a very pleasant route between hedges along the lower slope of Coombe Down. When you meet a road (the starting point for the next walk) a right turn will take you down into Ogbourne (**14**). St George's Café next stop! To continue on the Path turn to (**15**) on page 83.

Returning to Bishopstone

Bus 470 to Swindon (hourly Monday–Saturday; two-hourly Sunday afternoon), then Bus 475 to Bishopstone (an infrequent service, Monday–Saturday only).

Taxis: Ace, telephone: Swindon 38075; Calder, Swindon, telephone: Swindon 722222.

Staying in Ogbourne and Chiseldon

Wilderthorne House, Ogbourne St George, telephone: Ogbourne St George 201.

Mrs Cornfield, 5 High Street, Chiseldon, telephone: Swindon 740413.

Eating in Ogbourne

St George's Café.

Chapter 11

OGBOURNE ST GEORGE TO OVERTON HILL

9½ miles (15.25 km)

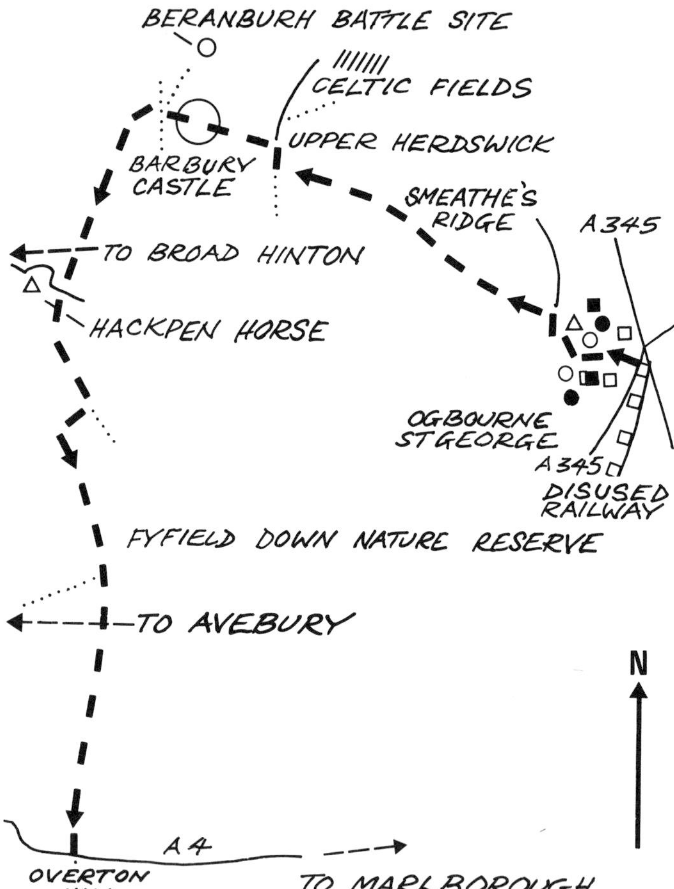

This final walk along the Ridgeway Path crosses the magnificent open landscape of the Marlborough Downs; a landscape typical of Wiltshire but unlike anything we have seen so far. Smeathe's Ridge, Barbury Castle, Hackpen Hill, Avebury Down – each an experience in itself.

At the far end of Ogbourne St George, near the church, stands March House with a magnificent chestnut tree on the front lawn. Here the road bends left. At the next bend (yesterday's point of arrival) a track going off left is signposted to Ogbourne St Andrew (**15**). *Do not* go down there but stay *on* the road for 100 yards (90 m) or so and turn left on to a concrete road. The road soon becomes a track and, after a few hundred yards, divides two ways. Take the left-hand branch through a gate and on to the open hillside. There is another gate ahead followed by two more ¼ mile (0.4 km) further on. The Path continues along the hillside, on a shelf-like feature at first, and then up to Smeathe's Ridge, overlooking a deep coombe on the left. Now you should correctly keep to the path close to the summit of the ridge, especially if the weather is grim and visibility poor. But if the day is good a short diversion to the edge of the coombe is well worthwhile for the sake of the view.

A stile beside a field gate sets you down on to a mile-long (1.6 km) path leading to a T-junction at Upper Herdswick, where there is a signpost giving directions to Barbury Castle and Marlborough. Turn right here and go past a bungalow and a farm. You should normally turn off left opposite the farm along a path signposted to Barbury Castle, but by continuing along what is now a made-up road to a field on the right you will have the opportunity to see a large sarsen stone inscribed in honour of Richard Jefferies and Alfred Williams. An extensive area of primitive cultivation fields, probably dating from Iron Age or Roman times, is laid downfield below the sarsen stone, on the north-facing slope of Burderop Down. They survive as little more than rectangular markings on the ground best seen from the road below.

By now you will have realized that Barbury Castle has been taken in hand by the planners, who have provided toilets, a car park, and an information kiosk. Since the kiosk fully describes the castle there is little to add except to point you to the site of a crucial battle that took place about AD 556 between the invading Saxons and the Romano-British inhabitants. If you climb the north-facing rampart of the castle you will see a small wooded enclosure, marked on the map as 'Beranburgh 556', about ½ mile (0.8 km) in the direction of Swindon. But let Alfred Williams paint the scene: 'Here the Britons, burning to avenge their defeat of a few years earlier, assembled a mighty host of their bravest warriors to oppose the Saxons. But neither choice of ground, nor the tradition of Roman tactics, nor heroic Celtic valour, could withstand the terrible impetuosity of the West Saxon Foot, and when the sun set, after a stout hand-to-hand fight that had lasted all day, Ceawlin was victor; the Kingdom of Wessex was firmly established.'

The Ridgeway Path runs through the centre of the castle and emerges at a break in the ramparts on the far side. It then descends to meet the Ridgeway proper at a multiway junction below. The barrows mentioned at the information kiosk are nearby. The disc barrow (which was probably for women) is on your right as you leave the castle; you will see this quite clearly later as you ascend Hackpen Hill. Two bowl barrows are quite evident at the junction itself. Now you should take the uphill track heading towards the massive beech clumps on Hackpen Hill. The Broad Hinton road is crossed 1½ miles (2.4 km) from Barbury. Here, but just out of sight of the Ridgeway, is Hackpen Horse, cut into the hillside. You can have sight of it by descending the road a short distance. The Horse was cut in 1838 by the parish clerk of nearby Broad Hinton to commemorate the coronation of Queen Victoria.

At a little more than 1 mile (1.6 km) along the Ridgeway you will arrive at a sharp right-hand turn; since you may have become accustomed to walking in a straight line a little caution is necessary. A track does indeed go straight on (through an iron gate) but you must *stay on the main track* as it turns right. After a few yards it turns left to resume its original direction. You will shortly pass a large sarsen stone beside the track: a token of the Ridgeway's entry into the prehistoric metropolis centred around Avebury. From here you can see the village of Avebury 2 miles (3.2 km) south-west in the Kennett valley. Avebury is partly enclosed by a great circle of sarsen stones brought from the hills on which you now stand. It is thought that the circle, together with two inner circles and a vast outer ditch, was constructed by immigrant Beaker peoples between the Late Stone Age and the Early Bronze Age (1800 BC or thereabouts), and used as an outdoor temple or ceremonial meeting place. Avebury is an attractive village in its own right and has a museum housing a collection of local archaeological finds.

If equipped with binoculars you will be able to see from this part of the Ridgeway an important archaeological site on Windmill Hill, some 2½ miles (4 km) eastward. The hill has given its name to an ancient culture that was brought to this country from the continent by a race of Neolithic men around 3000 BC. The site is formally classified as a Neolithic causewayed camp: it has – or rather had – three concentric circular ditches crossed at intervals by causeways. Opinions differ as to its function, but it seems likely that it was used either as an enclosure for cattle or pigs or as a trading centre. There is little to see from this distance and you may not be able to identify more than a small part of each circle; to confuse you, there are a few Bronze Age round barrows scattered across the site. For a closer view Windmill Hill can be reached from Avebury Trusloe or from the A361 road 1 mile (1.6 km) north of Avebury.

Continuing along the Ridgeway you will pass an entrance to Fyfield Down National Nature Reserve. Fyfield Down is 'one of the largest and finest unreclaimed tracts of high chalk grassland left in England'. Being an area noted for its many sarsen stones, which in themselves are of considerable interest, it is with good reason that the Down was set aside as a reserve by the Nature Conservancy in 1956. The reserve is noted for wild plants and animals that can take advantage of the relatively undisturbed environment. For the historian there is a wealth of interest in the primitive field systems which cover much of the reserve. Permits are normally required for visitors wishing to visit the reserve, other than along the public footpaths.

Overton Hill, the end of the Ridgeway Path, is now little more than 2 miles (3.2 km) away. Numerous barrows, many of them tree-covered, accompany the Path along this final stretch. The planting of trees on barrows and high points o the Downs was a fashionable nineteenth-century pastime; i served no practical purpose whatsoever and is understandabl deplored by archaeologists. Now to an important twentieth century settlement on the A4: the Ridgeway Café!

Opposite the café, on the south side of the A4, is the site of a Neolithic structure called The Sanctuary. All you will see are small concrete blocks marking the positions of holes whicl once held stones and wooden posts. The Sanctuary was linkec to the Avebury stone circle by the Kennett Avenue – ar avenue of stones that has now largely disappeared. The purpose of the Sanctuary can only be guessed at, but the possibility that it had some kind of ritualistic function canno be ruled out. It is very unfortunate that here, as elsewhere personal gain and short-sightedness brought destruction to a valuable archaeological site: in the nineteenth century a loca farmer was named as having removed the stones in order tc build a house in nearby Beckhampton. Even more incredible is the record of a Marlborough doctor who scoured the lanc hereabouts (presumably the barrows, of which there are many) for human remains. He ground the bones into powder and used this to produce what was, or so he claimed, a successful medicine.

Before going home you should take the opportunity to visit Avebury (bus 476 from West Kennett), Silbury Hill and the West Kennett long barrow. Avebury I have already mentioned. Silbury Hill is a massive mound beside the A4 1 mile (1.6 km) westward. With its 130-ft (40-m) summit and 5½-acre base it is the largest man-made mound in Europe – excluding slag heaps and the like, of course. The purpose of the hill is quite unknown; in spite of numerous excavations it has not revealed its secret. It was constructed in the late Neolithic period, about 2100 BC, and took an estimated 5000 man-years to build. Almost opposite Silbury Hill a path leads southwards from the A4 to the West Kennett long barrow — an important chambered tomb dating back to about 2700 BC.

Returning to Ogbourne St George

Bus 476 from West Kennett to Marlborough (Monday–Saturday, two-hourly), then Bus 470 to Ogbourne (Monday–Saturday, hourly, Sunday afternoon two-hourly). Taxis: Harley Hire Service, Marlborough, telephone: Marlborough 2786.

Staying in Overton Hill and Avebury

Ridgeway Café, Overton Hill, telephone: Lockeridge 234.
The Rectory, Avebury, telephone: Avebury 232.
Mrs Fry, Avebury, telephone: Avebury 362 (please phone before arriving).

APPENDIX

Rail and Bus Links with Towns on or Close to the Path

Tring
On the Euston–Bletchley line there is an hourly service. Tring station is on the Ridgeway Path, 1½ miles (2.4 km) from the own. Green Line coach 708 London (Victoria) to Tring runs very hour each day. Bus 61 links Tring (town) with Ivinghoe Beacon; this is an hourly service, two-hourly on Sundays.

Wendover
On the Marylebone–Aylesbury line there is an hourly service. On Sunday use the Metropolitan line from Baker Street, and change at Amersham.

Princes Risborough
On the Marylebone–Banbury line there is a two-hourly service Monday–Saturday but three-hourly on Sunday.

Goring and Streatley
On the Paddington–Oxford line there is an hourly service, one–three hourly on Sunday.

Swindon
This town is on the Paddington–Bristol/South Wales line. Bus 470 to Marlborough followed by 476 links Swindon with Overton Hill (East or West Kennett). 470 runs hourly Monday–Saturday, two-hourly Sunday afternoon. 476 runs wo-hourly Monday–Saturday only.

Bus Company Addresses
United Counties Omnibus Co. Ltd, Bedford Road, Northampton. Telephone: Northampton 35661. (Routes 61, 72, 366.)
London Country Bus Services Ltd, Lesbourne Road, Reigate, Surrey. Telephone: Reigate 42411. (Route 708.)
Alder Valley Omnibus Co. Ltd, 3 Thorne Walk, Reading, Berks. Telephone: Reading 54046. (Routes 112, 323, 324.)

City of Oxford Motor Services Ltd, 395 Cowley Road Oxford. Telephone: Oxford 774611. (Routes 302, 304, 390.) Chiltern Queens Ltd, Woodcote, Reading, Berks. Telephone Checkendon 680354. (Route B.)
Bristol Omnibus Co. Ltd, Berkeley House, Lawrence Hill Bristol. Telephone: Bristol 558211. (Routes 470, 475, 476. House's Watlington Buses, Watlington, Oxon. Telephone Watlington 2319.

Note

Rail and Bus services given throughout this guide are subjec to change and you would be well advised to check on route and times before setting out.

Early Closing Days

Tuesday: South Stoke.
Wednesday: Ivinghoe, Tring, Wendover, Princes Risborough Watlington, Wallingford, Goring, Swindon, Marlborough.
Thursday: Streatley, Wantage.
Saturday: Bishopstone.

BIBLIOGRAPHY

Portrait of Buckinghamshire, by John Camp (Hale).

Berkshire, by Ian Yarrow (Hale).

Companion into Buckinghamshire, by Maxwell Fraser (Spurbooks).

Companion into Berkshire, by R. P. Beckinsale (Spurbooks).

Villages of the White Horse, by Alfred Williams (Duckworth, 1913).

Chiltern Country, by H. J. Massingham (Batsford, 1940).

English Downland, by H. J. Massingham (Batsford, 1936).

Chalkways of South and South-East England, by Edward C. Pyatt (David and Charles).

The Icknield Way, by Anthony Bulfield (Dalton).

The Chilterns, British Landscape Through Maps, by J. T. Coppock (Geographical Association).

The Living Land, A Natural History of the Chiltern Hills, by Michael Smith (Spurbooks).

The Birds of Berkshire and Oxfordshire, by M. C. Radford (Longman).

Wild Flowers of Chalk and Limestone, by J. E. Louseley (Collins).

Discovering Regional Archaeology series: *Eastern England,* by James Dyer, and *Wessex,* by Leslie Grinsell and James Dyer (Shire Publications).

Buildings of England series: *Buckinghamshire, Berkshire, Oxfordshire, Wiltshire,* by Nikolaus Pevsner (Penguin Books).

White Horses and other Hill Figures, by Morris Marples (S. R. Publications Ltd).

The Oldest Road – An Exploration of the *Ridgeway,* by J. R. L. Anderson and Fay Godwin (Wildwood House).